Lewis E. Jackson, N.Y. City Mission and Tract Society

**Gospel Work in New York City**

a memorial of fifty years in city missions

Lewis E. Jackson, N.Y. City Mission and Tract Society

**Gospel Work in New York City**
*a memorial of fifty years in city missions*

ISBN/EAN: 9783337285739

Printed in Europe, USA, Canada, Australia, Japan

Cover: Foto ©Lupo / pixelio.de

More available books at **www.hansebooks.com**

# Gospel Work

IN

# NEW YORK CITY.

## *A MEMORIAL*

OF

## FIFTY YEARS IN CITY MISSIONS.

BY LEWIS E. JACKSON,
CORRESPONDING SECRETARY.

*NEW YORK CITY MISSION,*
50 BIBLE HOUSE.
*1878.*

"Our fathers have told us, what work thou didst in their days: showing to the generation to come the praises of the LORD." Psa. 44:1; 78:4.

"Cast thy bread upon the waters: for thou shalt find it after many days." Eccles. 11:1.

———•———

"Sow thy seed, be never weary,
   Let no fears thy soul annoy;
Be the prospect ne'er so dreary,
   Thou shalt reap the fruits of joy."

# CONTENTS.

|     |                                      |     |
| --- | ------------------------------------ | --- |
| I.    | Historical ........PAGE             | 5   |
| II.   | Anniversaries                        | 24  |
| III.  | Year by Year                         | 38  |
| IV.   | Tracts distributed                   | 53  |
| V.    | Plans and Methods                    | 55  |
| VI.   | A Missionary Report                  | 63  |
| VII.  | What it costs                        | 65  |
| VIII. | Personal Effort                      | 67  |
| IX.   | Fruitfulness of Fruit                | 68  |
| X.    | Hope for Drunkards                   | 71  |
| XI.   | Tract Work                           | 75  |
| XII.  | How to help the Poor                 | 78  |
| XIII. | What can I do?                       | 81  |
| XIV.  | The Soul that stands next            | 86  |
| XV.   | Doing One's Duty                     | 88  |
| XVI.  | Take a Stand                         | 92  |
| XVII. | Danger of Neglecting one Child       | 94  |

## CONTENTS.

| | | |
|---|---|---|
| XVIII. | How to save Souls | 99 |
| XIX. | A Mission Convert becomes a Missionary | 100 |
| XX. | Scandinavians—The Cosmopolitan City | 104 |
| XXI. | Living and Teaching the Gospel of Christ | 108 |
| XXII. | Water Street | 112 |
| XXIII. | The Masses | 114 |
| XXIV. | Coöperation | 117 |
| XXV. | Workingmen's Clubs | 120 |
| XXVI. | Tenement Houses | 122 |
| XXVII. | Our Danger | 130 |
| XXVIII. | Tried and Proved | 134 |
| XXIX. | Testimonies | 139 |
| XXX. | Woman's Work | 148 |
| XXXI. | Organization—Constitution—By-Laws—Chapels—Services—Carmel Chapel—Olivet Chapel—Helping Hand—Honorary Members—Officers—Missionaries—Present Status—Church Organization—Form of Reporting—Corporate Titles—Forms of Bequest | 165 |

# Gospel Work

IN

# NEW YORK CITY.

## I.

### *HISTORICAL.*

Fifty years of Gospel work, in the city of New York, having been successfully completed, and there being a constant call for information as to the plans and results of the same, the present volume has been prepared, with a view of preserving in convenient shape the leading facts in the formation of the City Mission, with such additional statements as will serve to exhibit its aims, its practical operations, and some of its more important results. A concise statement of the history of the City Mission will appear in a brief recital of the several salient points in its organization and development.

In the "Commercial Advertiser" of Monday,

February 19, 1827, there appeared the following notice:

"A public meeting will be held at the City Hotel this evening, at 7½ o'clock, for the purpose of forming a New York City Tract Society, for the supply of our seamen, our Humane and Criminal Institutions, and for other local tract operations in this city. Several addresses will be delivered. A general attendance of all who are friendly to the object is requested."

In the same paper, on the following Wednesday, there was found this brief report:

"TRACT SOCIETY.—Agreeably to public notice, a large assemblage of ladies and gentlemen convened on Monday evening at the City Hotel, for the purpose of organizing a society to be called the 'Tract Society of New York, auxiliary to the American Tract Society.' Richard Varick, Esq., presided, and the meeting was addressed by the Rev. Mr. Somers, the Rev. Mr. Monteith, Rev. Dr. Milnor, Rev. Dr. Macauley, and two other gentlemen, agents of the American Tract Society. The Constitution was read and adopted, after which many of those present became subscribers to the new Constitution."

From a more extended report in the "New York Observer," of Saturday, February 24, it appeared that in addition to those named above, the Rev. Dr. Knox, the Rev. Dr. Brodhead, and the Rev. Dr. Spring, also actively participated in the proceedings, and that the Rev. W. A. Hallock acted as Secretary, who also read the report of a preliminary meeting which had been held on the 7th, and presented the draft of the Constitution as it had been prepared by a Committee selected for that purpose.

The ministers and the laymen taking part in this meeting were of different churches, of various denominations, and their basis of action was their general agreement with the evangelical faith, and their single aim to make the gospel known to the multitudes outside of the churches.

The Officers and Directors of the NEW YORK CITY TRACT SOCIETY for the first year were as follows:

*President*—ZECHARIAH LEWIS.

*Vice-Presidents*—Rev. JOHN STANFORD, Rev. CAVE JONES, Rev. HENRY CHASE, Dr. JOHN NEILSON, Dr. JOHN STEARNS, THOMAS STOKES, GERARD BEEKMAN, and ARTHUR TAPPAN.

*Corresponding Secretary*—GERARD HALLOCK.

*Recording Secretary*—OLIVER E. COBB.

*Treasurer*—RALPH V. BEEKMAN.

*Directors*—JOHN ALEXANDER, MOSES ALLEN, AUGUSTIN AVERILL, MICAH BALDWIN, JAMES BAKER, ISAAC BEACH, ELI BENEDICT, Dr. JAMES C. BLISS, A. BAKER, JOSEPH BREWSTER, REUBEN BRUMLEY, FREDERICK BULL, JIREH BULL, E. K. BUSSING, W. W. CHESTER, ELISHA COIT, O. E. COBB, WM. R. COOK, RICHARD CUNNINGHAM, RUFUS DAVENPORT,

John S. Davenport, Rev. Austin Dickinson, William E. Dodge, George Douglass, Wm. R. Dwight, Charles M. Dwight, Wm. W. Edwards, Alfred Edwards, Stephen Griggs, Charles Hall, William Hall, Rev. Wm. A. Hallock, Timothy Hedges, John W. Hinton, John D. Holbrook, Fisher How, Joseph Howard, Jonas Humbert, E. D. Hurlbut, Joseph Hurlbut, Rev. Albert Judson, John Ledyard, George Marsh, Rev. W. G. Miller, John Moir, Wm. D. Murphy, Jacob C. Mott, Edward H. Neilson, Elias Nexsen, Jr., Peter Ogilvie, Ralph Olmstead, Joseph Otis, Anson G. Phelps, Zephaniah Platt, William Poe, Capt. C. Prince, John Rankin, James B. Requa, Peter R. Roach, George P. Shipman, Lewis Tappan, Knowles Taylor, Henry E. Thomas, W. R. Thompson, A. S. Thornton, Abraham Van Horne, Samuel G. Wheeler, John Wheelwright, Jeremiah Wilbur, and Timothy D. Williams.

During the first year, the Society distributed, through the agency of its committees and volunteer visitors, 2,368,548 pages, equal to 592,137 tracts of four pages each, and received and expended the sum of $2,090 86, and commenced the second year with a balance in the treasury of $24.

For six or seven years following, the Society

continued its useful operations in the same line, gradually growing in strength and efficiency. Such was the success attending these efforts, and so many providential openings were discovered for increased exertion, that it was deemed best to engage men as missionaries who should devote their whole time to Christian efforts among the poor and neglected. Accordingly, in 1833, mainly through the liberality of two or three individuals, men were set to work in the Fifth and Eighth Wards; and subsequently, in 1835, the employment of missionaries became the policy of the Society, and the number of missionaries was increased to fourteen. In the same year, viz., 1835, the Society held two Annual Meetings; the first being held March 11, 1835; and the second, December 23, 1835; and from the last date onward, the Annual Meeting has been held in December, and is now fixed by the charter for the Wednesday following the second Monday in December of each year. And this will explain why the Fiftieth Anniversary, which would properly fall on February 19, 1877, is celebrated two months earlier.

For thirty years the Tract Missionaries, as they were generally called, carried forward their evangelistic operations, bringing the neglecters of the sanctuary into the churches, the children into Sabbath-schools, and holding prayer-meetings in destitute neighborhoods, etc., and during this period they reported an aggregate of tracts distributed, 30,000,000; of conversions, 7,000; and money expended, $400,000.

In 1864 steps were taken looking to the reorganization of the Society; new men were brought into the Board of Directors, an office was rented in the Bible House, a Secretary was appointed, who was to devote his whole time to writing up the history of the Society, and to giving information to the public. And now commenced the publication of the reports and papers on the methods and results of city evangelization, which have had much to do with awaking and directing Christian zeal and activity in this and in other cities, in labors among the lowly; so that the office of the City Mission has come to be recognized as a bureau of information on church and charitable work generally, and applications for plans of operations and illustrative facts and arguments are constantly being received from all parts of the country.

One of the secretary's articles, published in the "Journal of Commerce," May, 1864, drew out an unexpected response from a gentleman, who gave

$5,000 towards the establishment of a fund for building mission chapels, which fund soon after reached the sum of $100,000.

At the thirty-eighth annual meeting, Dec. 14, 1864, the name of the Society was changed to that of the New York City Mission and Tract Society. In 1866 the Society was incorporated by the state legislature, and in the same year a Superintendent of Missions was appointed for the organization of mission chapels and services, the instruction of the missionaries, and the advocacy of the claims of the Society in the churches and Sabbath-schools.

In 1867 the first of the chapels, now known as Olivet Chapel, was built on a piece of ground in the interior of the block between First and Second streets, and First and Second avenues; the ground belonged to the First Street Presbyterian Church, then recently disbanded, and was given, with some personal property, to the City Mission by the trustees thereof, for that purpose—the state legislature by special act authorizing the trustees so to do, and thereby confirming the City Mission in their title to the possession of the property.

At the same time premises were rented or purchased in various other parts of the city, in which mission stations were established. Simultaneously with these movements, individual churches and denominational unions also actively engaged in similar evangelistic enterprises, and the number of mission chapels was greatly increased. And as the churches generally located their missions in the upper parts of the city, the City Mission felt it to be their province to care particularly for the more neglected portions of the city lying chiefly below Fourteenth street.

With commodious and attractive chapels established and regularly ordained ministers appointed thereunto, the preaching of the gospel and other religious services were appointed, Sabbath-schools, temperance meetings, helping hands, and other appliances, were instituted, and multitudes were brought under the influence of the truth. Through the Divine blessing resting on and following these labors many souls were hopefully converted. In the earlier years of the tract effort the tract missionaries and their visitors led their converts into the various churches. Now, at least in many instances, there were no churches at hand where the converts could easily go; and naturally feeling a strong attachment to those who first sought them out, and to the chapel which had become their spiritual birthplace, these converts expressed an earnest desire to be gathered into a church on the ground.

For two or three years the question of church organization was agitated, until the Executive Committee, who had minute and careful oversight of all the operations of the missionaries and the workings of the chapels, were fully persuaded that the time had come when the proper care and growth of the converts gathered by the missionaries demanded the administration of the Christian ordinances in the mission chapels. After mature deliberation the Executive Committee resolved to lay the matter before the Society, which was done at the annual meeting held Dec. 15, 1869, when, after a free and general interchange of views, the Society authorized the Executive Committee to proceed to the formation of Christian congregations in the several mission chapels, as called for.

The following plan was adopted for the orderly introduction of the Christian ordinances into the City Mission chapels:

1. A committee of the Executive Committee shall be appointed to visit the mission chapel, and those persons who shall wish to unite in the Christian society there to be formed, shall present to this committee the evidence of their piety, either by certificate of their church-membership, or by examination before the committee, and when approved by the committee they shall form the Christian Society of said mission.

2. The Society thus defined shall immediately proceed to elect, by a majority of all its members, in which of the forms recognized among evangelical Christians the ordinances shall be observed within it, and this decision shall be irreversible in that Society, except by a vote of three-fourths of all its members.

3. It shall then be submitted to the Society whether they will elect four or six officers, in classes of two each, to whom shall be committed the duty of examining, under the counsel of the missionary in charge, and receiving all additional members, and of excluding from the ordinances those who, after a fair investigation, shall be found to be unworthy of them.

4. If such election be determined upon, it shall at once proceed. The officers of the second class then elected shall hold office for one year, when there shall be an election of an equal number of officers to take their place. The officers of the first class shall be replaced by an election to be held two years hence, and yearly elections shall be held thereafter, in such manner that all officers shall serve two years. The officers who shall have completed their term of office shall be re-eligible.

5. These officers shall have a spiritual oversight of the members of the Society, but they shall have no control of any of those details of mission work which have hitherto been within the power of the Executive Committee. The discipline which they shall administer shall conform to rules to be hereafter drawn out by the Executive Committee.

6. When any convert who shall wish to join the Society thus constituted shall have conscientious preferences in behalf of any form of baptism in use among evangelical Christians, that ordinance shall be administered in his case according to such preference. And when so many as five members of such Society shall have conscientious preferences in behalf of any mode of administering the Lord's Supper which is in use among evangelical Christians, and is different from that which has been chosen by the Society, a special communion-service, according to such preference, shall be appointed for them, to occur as frequently as the service adopted by the Society,

7. The ordinances shall in each case be administered by an ordained minister, who shall be connected with some evangelical ecclesiastical body in this city or vicinity.

8. The Apostles' creed shall be adopted by the Society above described.

In 1870, in accordance with the action of the Society, and upon the plan adopted, Christian Societies were regularly organized in several of the mission chapels, and during the six years that have elapsed there have been received into membership, on the confession of their faith, an aggregate of 1,202 persons.

The Presidents of the Society have been: 1. ZECHARIAH LEWIS; 2. HON. THEODORE FRELINGHUYSEN; 3. Rev. JAMES MILNOR, D. D.; 4. Rev. THOMAS DE WITT, D. D.; and 5. A. R. WETMORE.

The office of Corresponding Secretary has been filled successively by, 1. GERARD HALLOCK; 2. SIDNEY E. MORSE; 3. JOHN CLEAVELAND; 4. JAMES F. ROBINSON; 5. Rev. CHARLES HYDE; 6. A. R. WETMORE; and 7. LEWIS E. JACKSON.

The Rev. GEORGE J. MINGINS was appointed Superintendent of Missions in 1866, and resigned in 1875.

The following is a list of those who have been in the missionary service of the Society, but are not now connected with it:

1. ADAMS, CHARLES.
2. AMBLER, J. L.
3. AMERMAN, R. S.
4. ABINGTON, M.
5. BABCOCK, W. R.
6. BACON, W. A.
7. BALLARD, J. B.
8. BATTERSBY, C.
9. BERGNER, PETER.
10. BERKY, ABRAHAM.
11. BETKER, JOHN P.
12. BISHOP, JAMES W.
13. BLATCHFORD, W. H.
14. BOUGHTON, PETER.
15. BRADFORD, WM.
16. BRADLEY, JOSEPH H.
17. BURDICK, JASON L.
18. BULEN, JOHN H.
19. BUTTS, JOSHUA.
20. BURI, PETER.
21. CAMP, AMZI.
22. CLEVELAND, HENRY W.
23. COE, NOAH.
24. COLLINS, CHARLES T.
25. CRAFT, CHARLES.
26. DARLING, CHARLES C.
27. DUBOIS, GEORGE.
28. DUBOIS, GRANT.
29. DICKHOUT, CONRAD.
30. ELMORE, JOHN B.
31. ENGLISH, ENEAS.
32. ERDMAN, M. A.
33. FINCH, MYRON.
34. FLETCHER, S.
35. FRASER, EDWARD A.
36. FRIEDEL, HENRY A.
37. FROST, S. A.
38. GELSTON, ROLAND.
39. GORY, ADRIAN.
40. GOSS, MARK.
41. GRAY, NATHANIEL.
42. GRAY, ROBERT H.
43. GRAY, WM.
44. GRIEVE, DAVID G.
45. GROSJEAN, GUSTAVUS.
46. GULDIN, JOHN C.
47. GULICK, THOMAS L.
48. HAGEN, F. F.
49. HALLIDAY, SAMUEL B.
50. HAWLEY, EDWIN H.
51. HARRIS, JOSEPH.
52. HARRIS, THOMAS T.
53. HAYTER, RICHARD.
54. HELLAND, OLA.
55. HOLT, WM. D.
56. HORTON, JONATHAN B.
57. HORTON, RICHARD.
58. HOWELLS, HENRY C.
59. HURLBUT, J. L.
60. HUTCHINSON, M. N.
61. HYDE, CHARLES.
62. JANES, FREDERICK.
63. JANES, WALTER R.
64. JONES, EDWIN F.
65. JONES, WM. B.
66. KIRBY, WM.
67. LATHROP, CALVIN.
68. LESTRADE, JOSEPH P.
69. LICHTENSTEIN, JOHN.
70. LITTLE, HENRY M.
71. LOCKWOOD, BENJAMIN.
72. LONGMORE, BENJAMIN.
73. LOVE, JOHN.
74. McDONALD, CHARLES.
75. McFARLAND, M.
76. MACK, ENOCH.
77. MARCHANT, HENRY.
78. MATTICE, HENRY.
79. MAY, EDWARD H.
80. MEACHAM, JOHN H.
81. METEER, JOHN H.
82. MARTIN, JOHN W.
83. MINGINS, GEORGE J.
84. MITCHELL, W. F.
85. MOORE, DAVID B.
86. MORLEY, S. B.
87. MUNROE, JAMES W.
88. NEFF, G.
89. NEWCOMB, CHARLES S.
90. NORTON, O. W.
91. ORCHARD, ISAAC.
92. OSTROM, JAMES I.
93. PARKER, RICHARD.
94. PETRESON, P.

## HISTORICAL.

95. PAYSON, EDWARD P.
96. PIERCEY, A. J.
97. POND, T.
98. PORTER, GEORGE.
99. POTTER, ALEX.
100. POWELL, C. H.
101. PRATT, EDWARD.
102. RAILSBACK, L.
103. ROBINSON, A. H.
104. ROE, ALFRED C.
105. ROTH, WM.
106. ROWLAND, LEVI P.
107. RUDY, JOHN.
108. RUSSELL, DAVID.
109. RUSSELL, SAMUEL.
110. SCHENCK, A. V. C.
111. SHARP, JOHN S.
112. SHELDRAKE, JOHN H.
113. SHIPMAN, D.
114. SHULTZ, E. M.
115. SMITH, WM. C.
116. SPANSWICK, THOMAS W.
117. SPENCER, P. A.
118. STANLEY, HENRY F.
119. STEINHART, J. A.
120. TERRY, DAVID.
121. TURNER, WM. S.
122. VAN DYKE, PETER.
123. VEHSLAGE, HENRY.
124. WARING, OSCAR M.
125. WEST, ROYAL.
126. WHITE, THOMAS.
127. WILDEY, JOSEPH.
128. WILDS, ZENAS P.
129. WITTELSEY, HENRY.
130. YOUNG, MICHAEL.
131. YOUNG, SAMUEL.

If to the foregoing we add the number now in the service, the aggregate will be 145, and if we still further add the number of missionary women who have been or are now in the work, the grand total will reach 200.

The money expended in sustaining the missionaries and carrying on the operations of the Society, by the several decades, appears as follows:

1827 to 1837, $41,761 39.
1837 to 1847, 104,833 35.
1847 to 1857, 148,496 60.
1857 to 1867, $199,805 69.
1867 to 1877, 450,620 59.

Adding to the above the sum of $100,000 expended in building mission chapels, we have the grand aggregate of $1,045,517 62.

The summary of results for the fifty years appears as follows, it being borne in mind that the full records only cover a period of forty-two years, the practice of reporting being first systematically arranged in 1835.

| | |
|---|---:|
| Years of missionary labor | 1,104 |
| Missionary visits | 2,104,751 |
| Tracts in English and other languages distributed | 42,720,893 |
| Bibles and Testaments supplied to the destitute | 86,052 |
| Volumes loaned | 166,851 |
| Children gathered into Sabbath-schools | 109,317 |
| Children gathered into day-schools | 23,303 |
| Persons gathered into Bible-classes | 14,274 |
| Persons induced to attend church | 223,085 |
| Temperance pledges obtained | 50,054 |
| Religious meetings held | 110,927 |
| Persons restored to church-fellowship | 3,074 |
| Persons hopefully converted | 21,650 |
| Converts united with evangelical churches | 12,972 |

From these records it will appear that the hopeful conversions have averaged 500 per year, which would make an aggregate of 25,000 hopeful conversions for the entire period of fifty years. And for the same length of time there have been 300 additions to the churches each year, making an aggregate of 15,000 added during the fifty years. And the amount expended in carrying on the operations of the Society has averaged $20,000 a year, which, for the fifty years, makes a total of $1,000,000.

In this historical review notice should be made

of the work of the Female Branch. It appears that the incipient steps in the formation of this auxiliary were taken in consultations held at the house of Mrs. Divie Bethune (daughter of Isabella Graham) in 1822. The Constitution was reported and organization completed in its first public meeting, which was held in the Brick Church Chapel, Park Row, March 25, 1822. In 1827 it was resolved, in view of the extent of the field presented before the Female Tract Society, and the great need of increased effort, to employ a woman, at least for part of her time, as an agent; and this resolution was immediately acted upon, and a woman was appointed, who, at the end of her first month's labor, reported visits to ninety families and calls upon several clergymen in reference to forming auxiliary tract associations in their churches. This may be said to have been the first step in woman's work in city missions. But the idea thus originated seems to have been of slow growth, and no further definite action in that direction appears upon the records until the year 1854, when a good woman, who had shown great zeal and skill as a volunteer tract visitor, was employed at a small salary to devote her whole time to systematic visitation among the poor and needy; and within a year or two other women were set to work, until 1856, when there were four regularly employed.

In 1863, the Female Branch, whose contributions had previously gone to the payment of the bills for the tracts used in distribution, resolved that henceforth their work should be directed to the raising of money for the support of the missionary women.

In 1875, the Female Branch was reorganized; the Board of Managers constituted five of their number an Executive Committee, to give particular attention to the business details; and a Superintendent was appointed, to give instruction and direction to the missionary women, receive applications for appointment, write up the history of the work, address appeals to the benevolent ladies of the city, etc. Within the two years that have elapsed, the amount of contributions and the number of missionaries have been doubled. And during the last year a house has been taken, where the missionaries may have the comforts of a home and enjoy the benefits of proper supervision, and a systematic training for their work.

Having thus presented an historical statement of the successive steps in the organization of the NEW YORK CITY MISSION AND TRACT SOCIETY, from the beginning, in 1827, and exhibited some of the results of the fifty years that have elapsed, it is believed that the friends of the cause will find herein occasion for devout thanksgiving to Almighty God for his providential care of the work and the workmen, and for the blessing that has followed their labors, and will be encouraged still to continue to them their generous confidence and support. The City Mission of to-day is settled substantially on the same basis of Christian union and coöperation as at the first, and has the same object in view, viz., the evangelization of the people not otherwise reached by the churches. It is the auxiliary of the churches, going out after those ready to perish. It is the helper of the churches in a most difficult and yet necessary work, and should receive the liberal aid of all the friends of Christ.

Pastors and churches of various denominations have frequently testified to the economy and efficiency of this instrumentality, and the Presbytery of New York, representing the majority of the friends and supporters of this Society, unanimously passed the following resolution:

"The Presbytery of New York, recognizing the NEW YORK CITY MISSION AND TRACT SOCIETY as an important auxiliary of the church for carrying the gospel to the destitute, would commend the same to the confidence of the churches, and bespeak for it the prayers and active coöperation of all."

The work of the Society, as now arranged, comprehends Gospel Services, Gospel Temperance Meetings, Sabbath-Schools, Bible-Classes, Reading-Rooms, and various auxiliary contrivances, all aiming at the one grand design of making the gospel known to the multitudes of men, women, and children not otherwise reached by the churches.

At the present time a fresh interest is manifest in the condition of the poor in tenement-houses, and renewed efforts are being made in the way of, 1. Improving Tenement-Houses, and 2. Providing Missionary Nurses for the Sick Poor.

Another project is that of Workingmen's Clubs, designed, not to add to the charities of New York, but to furnish workingmen with healthy moral, Christian forms of entertainment and instruction, and places of resort where they may be free from the vicious and degrading influences of the drinking places. And still another scheme is to give men out of work a chance to help themselves, by purchasing a farm convenient to the city, and setting them to work thereon. The laborers in City Missions constantly see their work growing in importance, and believe that it is intimately connected with all the best interests of society, and deserves the earnest, thoughtful consideration and hearty support of every good citizen.

To disarm Communism, to expose the errors of Rationalism and Materialism, is needed the widest diffusion of that practical Christianity which teaches all men to bear one another's burdens, directs the strong to help the weak, and commands us to fulfil the law of Christ, who received publicans and sinners, and was the considerate friend of those who were ignorant and out of the way

The City Mission, as the representative of the churches, is going down into the depths of poverty and ignorance and vice, and is daily illustrating, in its deeds of love and sympathy, the unselfish spirit of the gospel, and furnishing fresh arguments for the truth of Christianity, and new proofs of its Divine origin and power. And as the churches shall continue to support and strengthen this instrumentality will its means and appliances be made effective for dispersing the darkness of ignorance and sin and error, and leading souls into the light of life.

## II.

### ANNIVERSARIES OF THE CITY MISSION.

1828, February 6, Wednesday evening. The first Anniversary held in the Masonic Hall, Broadway, near Pearl street, opposite the New York Hospital. The President Mr. Zechariah Lewis, Rev. Mr. Stanford, Dr. John Stearns, Mr. Gerard Hallock, Mr. Zephaniah Platt, Rev. W. A. Hallock, Rev. C. P. McIlvaine, Mr. Timothy Hedges, and Rev. Dr. James Milnor participated in the proceedings.

1829, February 4, Wednesday evening. The second Anniversary held in the Masonic Hall, Broadway, near Pearl street. The President Mr. Zechariah Lewis, Rev. Cyrus Mason, Mr. Alfred Edwards, Mr. Gerard Hallock, Rev. H. G. Ludlow, Mr. Jeremiah Evarts, Rev. T. E. Vermilye, Rev. W. A. Hallock, and Rev. David Temple participated in the services.

1830, February 3, Wednesday evening. The third Anniversary held in the Masonic Hall, Broadway, near Pearl street. Dr. John Stearns, Vice-President, Rev. Cyrus Mason, Rev. W. A. Hallock, Mr. Lewis Tappan, Mr. Sidney E. Morse, Rev. Dr.

Jacob Brodhead, Rev. Benjamin H. Rice, Rev. Dr. Gardiner Spring, Rev. Dr. John Knox, Rev. William Patton, and Rev. Dr. Thomas De Witt participated in the proceedings.

1831, April 18, Monday evening. The Fourth Anniversary held in the Masonic Hall, Broadway, near Pearl street. The President Mr. Zechariah Lewis, Rev. W. A. Hallock, Mr. Sidney E. Morse, Rev. Peter Stryker, Rev. Dr. James Milnor, Rev. Sylvester Woodbridge, Mr. Lewis Tappan, and Rev. Dr. Samuel H. Cox participated in the proceedings.

1832, March 14, Wednesday evening. The Fifth Anniversary held in the Masonic Hall, Broadway, near Pearl street. The Rev. A. Maclay, Rev. W. A. Hallock, Mr. S. E. Morse, Rev. Charles Hyde, Mr. S. B. Halliday, Rev. Joel Parker, Rev. Charles G. Sommers, Rev. Dr. Robert McCartee, Mr. A. Van Sinderen, Rev. O. Eastman, Rev. Edward Beecher, and Rev. Benjamin H. Rice participated in the proceedings.

1833, March 13, Wednesday evening. The sixth Anniversary held in the Chatham Street Chapel, Chatham, near Pearl street. The President Mr. Zechariah Lewis, Rev. Dr. John Knox, Mr. Jesse Talbot, Mr. J. F. Robinson, Rev. Dr. McMurray,

Mr. Edward Probyn, Rev. Dr. D. C. Lansing, Rev. B. C. Cutler, Rev. Wm. Patton, Mr. Moses Allen, and Rev. Dr. Woodbridge took part in the proceedings.

1834, April 16, Wednesday evening. The Seventh Anniversary was held in the Chatham Street Chapel. The President Mr. Zechariah Lewis, Rev. Dr. Thomas McAuley, Rev. O. Eastman, Mr. J. F. Robinson, Rev. David Bernard, Rev. Dr. Thomas De Witt, Rev. Mr. Green, Rev. H. G. Ludlow, and Rev. S. Woodbridge took part in the services.

1835, March 11. The Eighth Anniversary was held in the Chatham Street Chapel. The President Mr. Zechariah Lewis, Rev. C. G. Finney, Rev. O. Eastman, Mr. J. F. Robinson, Rev. William G. Miller, Rev. Asa D. Smith, Rev. William Adams, Rev. E. P. Barrows, and Rev. Dr. Samuel H. Cox took part in the services.

1835, December 23. The Ninth Anniversary was held in the Chatham Street Chapel. The President Mr. Zechariah Lewis, Rev. Wm. G. Miller, Mr. Alfred Edwards, Rev. Charles Hyde, Rev. Henry A. Rowland, Rev. E. F. Hatfield, Rev. M. S. Hutton, Rev. S. Woodbridge, and Rev. Dr. Gardiner Spring took part in the services.

1836, December 22. The Tenth Anniversary

was held in the Broadway Tabernacle, Broadway near Leonard street. The President Mr. Zechariah Lewis, Rev. Dr. John Knox, Mr. Alfred Edwards, Rev. O. Eastman, Rev. Sylvester Woodbridge, Rev. James W. McLane, Rev. W. R. Williams, Rev. E. N. Kirk, and Hon. Theodore Frelinghuysen took part in the services.

1837, December 20, Wednesday evening. The Eleventh Anniversary was held in the Broadway Tabernacle. The President Mr. Zechariah Lewis, Rev. Dr. Isaac Ferris, Mr. Alfred Edwards, Rev. O. Eastman, Rev. S. Woodbridge, Rev. Stephen Remington, Rev. J. W. Cooke, Rev. Silas Illsley, Rev. William Adams, Hon. J. S. Buckingham, and Rev. Dr. Thomas De Witt took part in the services.

1838, December 19, Wednesday evening. The Twelfth Anniversary was held in the Broadway Tabernacle. Mr. S. V. S. Wilder, Rev. Dr. Thomas De Witt, Rev. O. Eastman, Mr. Alfred Edwards, Rev. Isaac Orchard, Rev. Aaron Perkins, Rev. Dr. John Knox, Rev. David R. Downer, Rev. Dr. James Milnor, and Rev. Dr. Breckenridge took part in the services.

1839, December 18, Wednesday evening. The Thirteenth Anniversary was held in the Broadway Tabernacle The Hon. Theodore Frelinghuysen,

President, Rev. Dr. George Potts, Mr. Wm. Walker, Rev. O. Eastman, Rev. Isaac Orchard, Rev. W. W. Everts, Rev. Dr. Theodore E. Vermilye, Rev. E. N. Kirk, and Rev. Dr. James Milnor took part in the services.

1840, December 23. The Fourteenth Anniversary was held in the Broadway Tabernacle. The President Hon. Theodore Frelinghuysen, Rev. Henry Chase, Rev. O. Eastman, Mr. William Walker, Rev. Isaac Orchard, Rev. John O. Choules, Rev. M. S. Hutton, and Rev. Dr. Joel Parker took part in the services.

1841, December 22, Wednesday evening. The Fifteenth Anniversary was held in the Broadway Tabernacle. The President Hon. Theodore Frelinghuysen, Rev. E. W. Andrews, Mr. William Walker, Rev. R. S. Cook, Rev. Isaac Orchard, Rev. Elisha Tucker, Rev. E. S. Janes, Rev. William Adams, and Rev. Dr. Isaac Ferris took part in the services.

1842, December 21, Wednesday evening. The Sixteenth Anniversary was held in the Broadway Tabernacle. The President Hon. Theodore Frelinghuysen, Rev. Dr. W. W. Phillips, Mr. William Walker, Rev. R. S. Cook, Rev. Isaac Orchard, and Rev. David Bellamy took part in the services.

1843, December 20, Wednesday evening. The Seventeenth Anniversary was held in the Broadway Tabernacle. Mr. W. B. Crosby, Vice-president, Rev. Elisha Tucker, Mr. Wm. Walker, Rev. O. Eastman, Rev. Isaac Orchard, Rev. Dr. Noah Levings, Rev. James L. Hodge, Rev. Dr. John Scudder, and Rev. Geo. B. Cheever took part in the services.

1844, December 18, Wednesday evening. The Eighteenth Anniversary was held in the Broadway Tabernacle. The President the Rev. Dr. James Milnor, Rev. Dr. Thomas De Witt, Mr. William Walker, Rev. R. S. Cook, Rev. Isaac Orchard, Rev. Edward Lathrop, Rev. George Peck, Rev. Charles H. Read, and Rev. E. N. Kirk took part in the services.

1845, December 17, Wednesday evening. The Nineteenth Anniversary was held in the Broadway Tabernacle. Mr. Wm. B. Crosby, Vice-president, Rev. Dr. James W. Alexander, Mr. Wm. Walker, Rev. R. S. Cook, Rev. Isaac Orchard, Rev. John Dowling, Rev. Dr. M. S. Hutton, Rev. Dr. William Adams, Rev. Edward T. Taylor, and Rev. Dr. Thomas McAuley took part in the services.

1846, December 16, Wednesday evening. The Twentieth Anniversary was held in the Broadway Tabernacle. The President Rev. Dr. Thomas De

Witt, Rev. Dr. George Peck, Mr. William Walker, Rev. R. S. Cook, Rev. Isaac Orchard, Rev. S. A. Corey, Rev. Daniel Smith, Rev. Dr. Stephen H. Tyng, and Rev. W. W. Everts took part in the services.

1847, December 15, Wednesday evening. The Twenty-first Anniversary was held in the Broadway Tabernacle. The President Rev. Dr. Thomas De Witt, Rev. Dr. Gardiner Spring, Mr. Wm. Walker, Rev. R. S. Cook, Rev. Isaac Orchard, Rev. Ira R. Steward, Mr. Hiram Ketchum, and Rev. Henry Ward Beecher took part in the services.

1848, December 20, Wednesday evening. The Twenty-second Anniversary was held in the Broadway Tabernacle. The President Rev. Dr. Thomas De Witt, Rev. R. S. Cook, Mr. William Walker, Rev. Isaac Orchard, Rev. George F. Kettell, Rev. Dr. George W. Bethune, and Rev. Dr. Dill took part in the services.

1849, December 19, Wednesday evening. The Twenty-third Anniversary was held in the Broadway Tabernacle. The President Rev. Dr. Thomas De Witt, Rev. D. W. Clark, Mr. William Walker, Rev. R. S. Cook, Rev. Isaac Orchard, Rev. E. L. Magoon, Hon. Theodore Frelinghuysen, and Rev. Dr. William Adams took part in the services.

1850, December 18, Wednesday evening. The Twenty-fourth Anniversary was held in the Broadway Tabernacle. The President Rev. Dr. Thomas De Witt, Mr. William Walker, Rev. R. S. Cook, Rev. Isaac Orchard, Rev. Dr. James B. Hardenbergh, and Rev. Hugh Smith Carpenter took part in the services.

1851, December 17, Wednesday evening. The Twenty-fifth Anniversary was held in the Broadway Tabernacle. The President Rev. Dr. Thomas De Witt, Rev. William Bannard, Mr. William Walker, Rev. R. S. Cook, Rev. Isaac Orchard, Rev. James R. Stone, Rev. R. S. Foster, and Rev. Dr. Asa D. Smith took part in the services.

1852, December 15, Wednesday evening. The Twenty-sixth Anniversary was held in the Collegiate Reformed Dutch Church, Lafayette place, corner of Fourth street. The President Rev. Dr. Thomas De Witt, Rev. Dr. William Adams, Mr. William Walker, Rev. R. S. Cook, Rev. Isaac Orchard, Rev. Isaac Westcott, Rev. E. O. Haven, Rev. J. S. Lord, and Rev. G. L. Prentiss took part in the proceedings.

1853, December 14, Wednesday evening. The Twenty-seventh Anniversary was held in the Collegiate Reformed Dutch Church, Lafayette place, corner of Fourth street. Rev. Dr. Isaac Ferris, Vice-President, Rev. J. M. Reid, Mr. William Walker, Rev. O. Eastman, Rev. Isaac Orchard, Rev. A. D. Gillette, Rev. Theodore L. Cuyler, and Rev. A. A. Wood took part in the services.

1854, December 13, Wednesday evening. The Twenty-eighth Anniversary was held in the Collegiate Reformed Dutch Church, Lafayette place, corner of Fourth street. The President Rev. Dr. Thomas De Witt, Mr. William Walker, Rev. Dr. W. A. Hallock, Rev. Isaac Orchard, Rev. A. D. Gillette, Rev. J. M. Reid, and Rev. Dr. R. S. Storrs, Jr., took part in the services.

1855, December 19, Wednesday evening. The Twenty-ninth Anniversary was held in the Collegiate Reformed Dutch Church, Lafayette place, corner of Fourth street. The President Rev. Dr. Thomas De Witt, Rev. Dr. E. F. Hatfield, Mr. William Walker, Rev. R. S. Cook, Rev. Isaac Orchard, Rev. Joseph Banvard, Rev. Dr. John Thomson, and Rev. Hiram Mattison took part in the services.

1856, December 21, Sabbath evening. The Thirtieth Anniversary was held in the Reformed Dutch Church, Washington square. The Rev. Dr. Thomas De Witt, Mr. William Walker, Rev. O.

Eastman, Rev. Isaac Orchard, Rev. Dr. George W. Bethune, and Rev. Dr. Jesse T. Peck took part in the services.

1857, December 20, Sabbath evening. The Thirty-first Anniversary was held in the Madison Square Presbyterian Church. The Rev. Dr. William Adams, Vice-President, Rev. Edward Lathrop, D. D., Mr. S. W. Stebbins, Rev. Isaac Orchard, Rev. Dr. John McClintock, and Rev. H. D. Ganse took part in the services.

1858, December 19, Sabbath evening. The Thirty-second Anniversary was held in the Madison Square Presbyterian Church. The President Rev. Dr. Thomas De Witt, Rev. Dr. William Adams, Mr. William Walker, Mr. A. R. Wetmore, Rev. Isaac Orchard, Hon. W. C. Alexander, and Rev. A. Kingman Nott took part in the services.

1859, December 18, Sabbath evening. The Thirty-third Anniversary was held in the Collegiate Reformed Dutch Church, Fifth avenue and Twenty-ninth street. The President Rev. Dr. Thomas De Witt, Rev. Dr. Thomas E. Vermilye, Mr. A. R. Wetmore, Rev. Dr. Edward Lathrop, and Rev. Dr. W. J. Hoge took part in the services.

1860, December 16, Sabbath evening. The

Thirty-fourth Anniversary was held in the South Reformed Church, Fifth avenue and Twenty-first street. The President Rev. Dr. Thomas De Witt, Rev. Dr. John M. McAuley, Mr. William Walker, Mr. A. R. Wetmore, Rev. Thomas S. Hastings, Rev. Frederick G. Clark, and Rev. Dr. William Hague took part in the services.

1861, December 15, Sabbath evening. The Thirty-fifth Anniversary was held in the Madison Square Presbyterian Church. The President Rev. Dr. Thomas De Witt, Rev. Dr. Asa D. Smith, Mr. Wm. Walker, Mr. A. R. Wetmore, Rev. Dr. Robert R. Booth, Rev. Dr. H. G. Weston, and Rev. Dr. Wm. Adams, took part in the services.

1862, December 21, Sabbath evening. The Thirty-sixth Anniversary was held in the Madison Square Presbyterian Church. The President Rev. Dr. Thomas De Witt, Rev. Dr. Wm. Adams, Mr. Wm. Walker, Mr. A. R. Wetmore, Rev. H. B. Ridgaway, Rev. Joseph T. Duryea, and Rev. Dr. Thomas D. Anderson, took part in the services.

1863, December 20, Sabbath evening. The Thirty-seventh Anniversary was held in the Fifth Avenue Presbyterian Church, Fifth avenue and Nineteenth street. The Rev. Dr. N. L. Rice, Vice-president, Rev. Thos. S. Hastings, Mr. Wm. Walker, Mr. A. R. Wetmore, Rev. H. D. Ganse, and Rev. Alfred Cookman, took part in the services.

1864, December 14, Wednesday. The Thirty-eighth Annual Meeting for reports and elections was held in the Mission Rooms, Bible House. The Anniversary services were held on Sabbath evening, December 18, in the South Reformed Church, Fifth avenue and Twenty-first street. The Rev. Dr. N. L. Rice, Vice-president, Rev. Dr. W. G. T. Shedd, Mr. Lewis E. Jackson, and Rev. Dr. E. P. Rogers, took part in the services.

1865, December 13, Wednesday. The Thirty-ninth Annual Meeting for reports and elections was held in the Mission Rooms, Bible House. The Anniversary services were held in the Fourth Avenue Presbyterian Church, Sabbath evening, December 17. The President, Rev. Dr. Thomas De Witt, Rev. Dr. James O. Murray, Mr. Lewis E. Jackson, and Rev. Dr. Howard Crosby, took part in the services.

1866, December 12, Wednesday. The Fortieth Annual Meeting for reports and elections was held in the Mission Rooms, Bible House. A series of meetings were held in various churches during the year, and an Anniversary was held during the anniversary week, in May, in Irving Hall.

1867, December 11, Wednesday. The Forty-first Annual Meeting for reports and elections was held in the Mission Rooms, Bible House.

1868, December 16, Wednesday. The Forty-second Annual Meeting for reports and elections was held in the Mission Rooms, Bible House.

1869, December 15, Wednesday. The Forty-third Annual Meeting for reports and elections was held in the Mission Rooms, Bible House.

1870, December 14, Wednesday. The Forty-fourth Annual Meeting for reports and elections was held in the Mission Rooms, Bible House.

1871, December 13, Wednesday. The Forty-fifth Annual Meeting for reports and elections was held in the Mission Rooms, Bible House. Anniversary exercises were held the following Sabbath evening in the Fifth Avenue Presbyterian Church, Fifth avenue and Nineteenth street. And during the several years preceding there were many public meetings held in various churches, making known the plans and operations of city missions.

1872, December 11, Wednesday. The Forty-sixth Annual Meeting for reports and elections was held in the Mission Rooms, Bible House.

1873, December 10, Wednesday. The Forty-seventh Anniversary was held in Association Hall,

Fourth avenue and Twenty-third street. The President Rev. Dr. Thomas De Witt, Mr. A. R. Wetmore, Rev. George L. Shearer, Mr. Morris K. Jesup, Rev. George J. Mingins, Rev. Dr. John Hall, Rev. Dr. Joseph T. Duryea, Hon. Wm. E. Dodge, and Rev. Dr. Charles S. Robinson, took part in the services.

1874, December 16, Wednesday. The Forty-eighth Annual Meeting for reports and elections was held in the Mission Rooms, Bible House. And on the Sabbath evening following, December 20, anniversary services were held in the Broadway Tabernacle Church; the Rev. Dr. T. W. Chambers, Rev. Dr. Wm. M. Taylor, Rev. Dr. John Hall, and others, participating.

1875, December 15, Wednesday. The Forty-ninth Annual Meeting for reports and elections was held in the Mission Rooms, Bible House. On the Sabbath afternoon following, December 19, a sermon on City Evangelization was preached by the Rev. Dr. R. S. Storrs in the Fifth Avenue Presbyterian Church.

1876, December 13, Wednesday. The Fiftieth Anniversary was held in the Fourth Avenue Presbyterian Church; the President Mr. A. R. Wetmore, Rev. Dr. J. M. Stevenson, Mr. L. E. Jackson,

Rev. Dr. Wm. Ormiston, Rev. G. L. Shearer, Mr. S. B. Schieffelin, Mr. Z. S. Ely, Rev. S. B. Halliday, Mr. O. R. Kingsbury, Mr. Stephen Cutter, Rev. Richard Horton, Rev. George Hatt, Rev. Dr. Chas. S. Robinson, Rev. Dr. W. J. Tucker, and Rev. E. D. Murphy, participating in the services.

## III.
### YEAR BY YEAR.

#### 1827.
**FIRST YEAR.**

*President.*—ZECHARIAH LEWIS.
*Corresponding Secretary.*—GERARD HALLOCK.

**RESULTS.**

Distributed 592,127 tracts.
Receipts, $2,090 86.

#### 1828.
**SECOND YEAR.**

*President.*—ZECHARIAH LEWIS.
*Corresponding Secretary.*—GERARD HALLOCK.

**RESULTS.**

Distributed 530,299 tracts.
Receipts, $1,543 35.

#### 1829.
**THIRD YEAR.**

*President.*—ZECHARIAH LEWIS.
*Corresponding Secretary.*—SIDNEY E. MORSE.

**RESULTS.**

Distributed 593,683 tracts.
Receipts, $3,382 79.

## 1830.

### FOURTH YEAR.

*President.*—ZECHARIAH LEWIS.
*Corresponding Secretary.*—SIDNEY E. MORSE.

#### RESULTS.

Distributed 930,250 tracts.
Expended $5,673 03.

## 1831.

### FIFTH YEAR.

*President.*—ZECHARIAH LEWIS.
*Corresponding Secretary.*—SIDNEY E. MORSE.

#### RESULTS.

Distributed 622,374 tracts.
Expended $2,802 66.

## 1832.

### SIXTH YEAR.

*President.*—ZECHARIAH LEWIS.
*Corresponding Secretary.*—JOHN CLEAVELAND.

#### RESULTS.

Distributed 428,734 tracts.
Expended $5,218 78.

## 1833.

### SEVENTH YEAR.

*President.*—ZECHARIAH LEWIS.
*Corresponding Secretary.*—JAMES F. ROBINSON.

#### RESULTS.

Distributed 412,128 tracts.
Expended $1,733 48.
A Missionary employed part of the year.

## 1834.

### EIGHTH YEAR.

*President.*—ZECHARIAH LEWIS.
*Corresponding Secretary.*—JAMES F. ROBINSON.

#### RESULTS.

Distributed 396,429 tracts.
Expended $3,361 73.
Missionaries employed.

## 1835.

### NINTH YEAR—(part of year).

*President.*—ZECHARIAH LEWIS
*Corresponding Secretary.*—JAMES F. ROBINSON.

#### RESULTS.

Distributed 312,375 tracts.
Expended $6,816 32.
Fourteen Missionaries employed.

## 1835.

### NINTH YEAR (part of year).

*President.*—ZECHARIAH LEWIS.
*Corresponding Secretary.*—REV. CHARLES HYDE.

#### RESULTS.

Distributed 674,966 tracts.
Expended $9,138 39.
Fifteen Missionaries employed.

In 1835 there were two Annual Meetings held; the first, March 11, 1835; and the other, December 23, 1835, and from the last date onward the Annual Meeting has been held in December, and is now fixed by the Charter for the Wednesday following the second Monday in December in each year.

## 1836.

### TENTH YEAR.

*President.*—ZECHARIAH LEWIS.
*Corresponding Secretary.*—JAMES F. ROBINSON.

#### RESULTS.

Distributed 747,324 tracts.
Expended $10,562 81.
Sixteen Missionaries employed.

## 1837.

### ELEVENTH YEAR.

*President.*—ZECHARIAH LEWIS.
*Corresponding Secretary.*—A. R. WETMORE.

#### RESULTS.

Distributed 679,193 tracts.
Expended $10,229 19.
Fifteen Missionaries employed.

## 1838.

### TWELFTH YEAR.

*President.*—HON. THEO. FRELINGHUYSEN.
*Corresponding Secretary.*—A. R. WETMORE.

#### EESULTS.

Distributed 842,806 tracts.
Expended $10,655 05.
Fourteen Missionaries employed.

## 1839.

### THIRTEENTH YEAR.

*President.*—HON. THEO. FRELINGHUYSEN.
*Corresponding Secretary.*—A. R. WETMORE.

#### RESULTS.

Distributed 764,053 tracts.
Expended $10,607 10.
Fourteen Missionaries employed.

## 1840.

#### FOURTEENTH YEAR.

*President.*—HON. THEO. FRELINGHUYSEN.
*Corresponding Secretary.*—A. R. WETMORE.

##### RESULTS.

Distributed 684,599 tracts.
Expended $10,607 10.
Fourteen Missionaries employed.

## 1841.

#### FIFTEENTH YEAR.

*President.*—HON. THEO. FRELINGHUYSEN.
*Corresponding Secretary.*—A. R. WETMORE.

##### RESULTS.

Distributed 732,155 tracts.
Expended $11,075 00.
Fourteen Missionaries employed.

## 1842.

#### SIXTEENTH YEAR.

*President.*—REV. JAMES MILNOR, D. D.
*Corresponding Secretary.*—A. R. WETMORE.

##### RESULTS.

Distributed 778,614 tracts.
Expended $9,981 61.
Fourteen Missionaries employed.

## 1843.

#### SEVENTEENTH YEAR.

*President.*—REV. JAMES MILNOR, D. D.
*Corresponding Secretary.*—A. R. WETMORE.

##### RESULTS.

Distributed 848,571 tracts.
Expended $9,783 62.
Fourteen Missionaries employed.

## 1844.

**EIGHTEENTH YEAR.**

*President.*—REV. JAMES MILNOR, D. D.
*Corresponding Secretary.*—A. R. WETMORE.

### RESULTS.

Distributed 862,088 tracts.
Expended $10,065 31.
Seventeen Missionaries employed.

## 1845.

**NINETEENTH YEAR.**

*President.*—REV. JAMES MILNOR, D. D.
*Corresponding Secretary.*—A. R. WETMORE.

### RESULTS.

Distributed 1,001,853 tracts.
Expended $11,266 56.
Eighteen Missionaries employed.

## 1846.

**TWENTIETH YEAR.**

*President.*—REV. THOMAS DE WITT, D. D.
*Corresponding Secretary.*—A. R. WETMORE.

### RESULTS.

Distributed 1,024,170 tracts.
Expended $11,750 99.
Nineteen Missionaries employed.

## 1847.

**TWENTY-FIRST YEAR.**

*President.*—REV. THOMAS DE WITT, D. D.
*Corresponding Secretary.*—A. R. WETMORE.

### RESULTS.

Distributed 1,252,123 tracts.
Expended $13,997 70.
Twenty Missionaries employed.

## 1848.

#### TWENTY-SECOND YEAR.

*President.*—REV. THOMAS DE WITT, D. D.
*Corresponding Secretary.*—A. R. WETMORE.

#### RESULTS.

Distributed 1,308,433 tracts.
Expended $12,675 49.
Twenty Missionaries employed.

## 1849.

#### TWENTY-THIRD YEAR.

*President.*—REV. THOMAS DE WITT, D. D.
*Corresponding Secretary.*—A. R. WETMORE.

#### RESULTS.

Distributed 1,631,890 tracts.
Expended $13,049 12.
Twenty-one Missionaries employed.

## 1850.

#### TWENTY-FOURTH YEAR.

*President.*—REV. THOMAS DE WITT, D. D.
*Corresponding Secretary.*—A. R. WETMORE.

#### RESULTS.

Distributed 1,786,279 tracts.
Expended $13,649 46.
Twenty-six Missionaries employed.

## 1851.

#### TWENTY-FIFTH YEAR.

*President.*—REV. THOMAS DE WITT, D. D.
*Corresponding Secretary.*—A. R. WETMORE.

#### RESULTS.

Distributed 1,579,756 tracts.
Expended $15,776 76.
Twenty-six Missionaries employed.

## 1852.

### TWENTY-SIXTH YEAR.

*President.*—REV. THOMAS DE WITT, D. D.
*Corresponding Secretary.*—A, R. WETMORE.

#### RESULTS.

Distributed 1,359,403 tracts.
Expended $16,531 25.
Twenty-eight Missionaries employed.

## 1853.

### TWENTY-SEVENTH YEAR.

*President.*—REV. THOMAS DE WITT, D. D.
*Corresponding Secretary.*—A. R. WETMORE.

#### RESULTS.

Distributed 1,777,173 tracts.
Expended $17,722 18.
Twenty-six Missionaries employed.

## 1854.

### TWENTY-EIGHTH YEAR.

*President.*—REV. THOMAS DE WITT. D. D.
*Corresponding Secretary.*—A. R. WETMORE.

#### RESULTS.

Distributed 1,523,947 tracts.
Expended $16,879 07.
Twenty-six Missionaries employed.

## 1855.

### TWENTY-NINTH YEAR.

*President.*—REV. THOMAS DE WITT, D. D.
*Corresponding Secretary.*—A. R. WETMORE.

#### RESULTS.

Distributed 1,257,458 tracts.
Expended $16,464 58.
Thirty Missionaries employed.

## 1856.

### THIRTIETH YEAR.

*President.*—REV. THOMAS DE WITT, D. D.
*Corresponding Secretary.*—A. R. WETMORE.

#### RESULTS.

Distributed 1,183,671 tracts.
Expended $17,483 63.
Twenty-eight Missionaries employed.

## 1857.

### THIRTY-FIRST YEAR.

*President.*—REV. THOMAS DE WITT, D. D.
*Corresponding Secretary.*—A. R. WETMORE.

#### RESULTS.

Distributed 1,115,654 tracts.
Expended $17,986 36.
Thirty Missionaries employed.

## 1858.

### THIRTY-SECOND YEAR.

*President.*—REV. THOMAS DE WITT, D. D.
*Corresponding Secretary.*—A. R. WETMORE.

#### RESULTS.

Distributed 1,075,323 tracts.
Expended $17,378 15.
Thirty Missionaries employed.

## 1859.

### THIRTY-THIRD YEAR.

*President.*—REV. THOMAS DE WITT, D. D.
*Corresponding Secretary.*—A. R. WETMORE.

#### RESULTS.

Distributed 1,016,931 tracts.
Expended $17,109 96.
Twenty-eight Missionaries employed.

## 1860.

**THIRTY-FOURTH YEAR.**

*President.*—REV. THOMAS DE WITT, D. D.
*Corresponding Secretary.*—A. R. WETMORE.

### RESULTS.

Distributed 1,200,051 tracts.
Expended $17,227 92.
Thirty-two Missionaries employed.

## 1861.

**THIRTY-FIFTH YEAR.**

*President.*—REV. THOMAS DE WITT, D. D.
*Corresponding Secretary.*—A. R. WETMORE.

### RESULTS.

Distributed 1,013,783 tracts.
Expended $17,202 79.
Thirty-four Missionaries employed.

## 1862.

**THIRTY-SIXTH YEAR.**

*President.*—REV. THOMAS DE WITT, D. D.
*Corresponding Secretary.*—A. R. WETMORE.

### RESULTS.

Distributed 1,112,264 tracts.
Expended $18,100 00.
Thirty-four Missionaries employed.

## 1863.

### THIRTY-SEVENTH YEAR.

*President.*—REV. THOMAS DE WITT, D. D.
*Corresponding Secretary.*—A. R. WETMORE.

#### RESULTS.

Distributed 1,006,901 tracts.
Expended $21,855 01.
Thirty-four Missionaries employed.

At the Annual Meeting, December 20, 1863, Mr. Lewis E. Jackson was appointed the Corresponding Secretary.

## 1864.

### THIRTY-EIGHTH YEAR.

*President.*—REV. THOMAS DE WITT, D. D.
*Corresponding Secretary.*—LEWIS E. JACKSON.

#### RESULTS.

Eleven Mission Stations.
Thirty-seven Missionaries.
Expended $26,477 59.

At the Annual Meeting, December 14, 1864, the name of the Society was changed to that of the NEW YORK CITY MISSION AND TRACT SOCIETY.

## 1865.

### THIRTY-NINTH YEAR.

*President.*—REV. THOMAS DE WITT, D. D.
*Corresponding Secretary.*—LEWIS E. JACKSON.

#### RESULTS.

Eleven Mission Stations.
Forty-three Missionaries.
Expended $29,064 28.

## 1866.

### FORTIETH YEAR.

*President.*—REV. THOMAS DE WITT, D. D.
*Corresponding Secretary.*—LEWIS E. JACKSON.
*Sup't of Missions.*—REV. GEORGE J. MINGINS.

### RESULTS.

Fourteen Mission Station.
Forty-five Missionaries.
Expended $36,108 42.

The Society incorporated, February 19, 1866.
Lebanon Chapel opened, 1866.
Rev. George J. Mingins appointed Superintendent of Missions, 1866.

## 1867.

### FORTY-FIRST YEAR.

*President.*—REV. THOMAS DE WITT, D. D.
*Corresponding Secretary.*—LEWIS E. JACKSON.
*Sup't of Missions.*—REV. GEORGE J. MINGINS.

### RESULTS.

Fourteen Mission Stations.
Forty-six Missionaries.
Expended $44,691 79.
Olivet Chapel opened, 1867.

## 1868.

### FORTY-SECOND YEAR.

*President.*—REV. THOMAS DE WITT, D. D.
*Corresponding Secretary.*—LEWIS E. JACKSON.
*Sup't of Missions.*—REV. GEORGE J. MINGINS.

### RESULTS.

Twelve Mission Stations.
Forty-two Missionaries.
Expended $46,245 18.

## 1869.

### FORTY-THIRD YEAR.

*President.*—REV. THOMAS DE WITT, D. D.
*Corresponding Secretary.*—LEWIS E. JACKSON.
*Sup't of Missions.*—REV. GEORGE J. MINGINS.

#### RESULTS.

Ten Mission Stations.
Forty Missionaries.
Expended $53,188 26.

## 1870.

### FORTY-FOURTH YEAR.

*President.*—REV. THOMAS DE WITT, D. D.
*Corresponding Secretary.*—LEWIS E. JACKSON.
*Sup't of Missions.*—REV. GEORGE J. MINGINS.

#### RESULTS.

Seven Mission Stations.
Forty Missionaries.
Expended $50,556 86.
Calvary Chapel opened, 1870.
The Christian Ordinances administered in the Mission Chapel 1870.

## 1871.

### FORTY-FIFTH YEAR.

*President.*—REV. THOMAS DE WITT, D. D.
*Corresponding Secretary.*—LEWIS E. JACKSON.
*Sup't of Missions.*—REV. GEORGE J. MINGINS.

#### RESULTS.

Seven Mission Stations.
Forty Missionaries.
Expended $51,030 77.

## 1872.

### FORTY-SIXTH YEAR.

*President.*—REV. THOMAS DE WITT, D. D.
*Corresponding Secretary.*—LEWIS E. JACKSON.
*Sup't of Missions.*—REV. GEORGE J. MINGINS.

#### RESULTS.

Seven Mission Stations.
Forty Missionaries.
Expended $48,622 99.
Carmel Chapel opened, 1872.

## 1873.

### FORTY-SEVENTH YEAR.

*President.*—REV. THOMAS DE WITT, D. D.
*Corresponding Secretary.*—LEWIS E. JACKSON.
*Sup't of Missions.*—REV. GEORGE J. MINGINS.

#### RESULTS.

Seven Mission Stations.
Forty Missionaries.
Expended $42,687 28.
De Witt Chapel opened, 1873.

## 1874.

### FORTY-EIGHTH YEAR.

*President.*—REV. THOMAS DE WITT, D. D.
*Corresponding Secretary.*—LEWIS E. JACKSON.
*Sup't of Missions.*—REV. GEORGE J. MINGINS.

#### RESULTS.

Six Mission Stations.
Thirty Missionaries.
Expended $42,687 28.
Rev. Thomas De Witt, D. D., President, died 1874.

## 1875.

### FORTY-NINTH YEAR.

*President.*—A. R. WETMORE.
*Corresponding Secretary.*—LEWIS E. JACKSON.
*Sup't of Missions.*—REV. GEORGE J. MINGINS.
*Sup't of Female Department.*—MRS. A. R. BROWN.

### RESULTS.

Five Mission Stations.
Thirty Missionaries.
Expended $39,669 96.
Rev. George J. Mingins, Superintendent, resigned 1875.

## 1876.

### FIFTIETH YEAR.

*President.*—A. R. WETMORE.
*Corresponding Secretary.*—LEWIS E. JACKSON.
*Sup't of Female Department.*—MRS. A. R. BROWN.

### RESULTS.

Five Mission Stations.
Thirty-two Missionaries.
Expended $37,819 11.

## AGGREGATE.

### EXPENDITURES BY DECADES.

| | |
|---|---|
| 1827 to 1837 | $41,761 39 |
| 1837 to 1847 | 104,833 35 |
| 1847 to 1857 | 148,496 60 |
| 1857 to 1867 | 199,805 69 |
| 1867 to 1877 | 450,620 59 |
| | $945,517 62 |
| Building fund | 100,000 00 |
| | $1,045,517 62 |

Equal to $20,000 per year for the whole period of fifty years, and for the last ten years, presenting an average of $50,000 per year.

## IV.

## TRACTS DISTRIBUTED AND MONEY EXPENDED.

|  |  | Distributed. | Expended. |
|---|---|---|---|
| 1827 | 1st year | 592,127 tracts | $2,090 86 |
| 1828 | 2d " | 530,299 " | 1,543 35 |
| 1829 | 3d " | 593,683 " | 3,382 79 |
| 1830 | 4th " | 930,250 " | 5,673 03 |
| 1831 | 5th " | 622,374 " | 2,802 66 |
| 1832 | 6th " | 428,734 " | 5,218 78 |
| 1833 | 7th " | 412,128 " | 1,733 48 |
| 1834 | 8th " | 396,429 " | 3,361 73 |
| 1835 | 9th " | 987,341 " | 15,954 71 |
| 1836 | 10th " | 747,324 " | 10,562 81 |
| 1837 | 11th " | 679,193 " | 10,229 19 |
| 1838 | 12th " | 842,806 " | 10,655 05 |
| 1839 | 13th " | 764,053 " | 10,607 10 |
| 1840 | 14th " | 684,599 " | 10,607 10 |
| 1841 | 15th " | 732,155 " | 11,075 00 |
| 1842 | 16th " | 778,614 " | 9,981 61 |
| 1843 | 17th " | 848,571 " | 9,783 62 |
| 1844 | 18th " | 862,088 " | 10,065 31 |
| 1845 | 19th " | 1,001,853 " | 11,266 56 |
| 1846 | 20th " | 1,024,170 " | 11,750 99 |
| 1847 | 21st " | 1,252,123 " | 13,997 70 |
| 1848 | 22d " | 1,308,433 " | 12,675 49 |
| 1849 | 23d " | 1,631,890 " | 13,049 12 |
| 1850 | 24th " | 1,786,279 " | 13,649 46 |
| 1851 | 25th " | 1,579,756 " | 15,776 76 |
| 1852 | 26th " | 1,359,403 " | 16,531 25 |

|  |  | Distributed. |  | Expended. |  |
|---|---|---|---|---|---|
| 1853 | 27th year | 1,777,173 tracts | | 17,722 | 18 |
| 1854 | 28th " | 1,523,947 | " | 16,879 | 07 |
| 1855 | 29th " | 1,257,458 | " | 16,464 | 58 |
| 1856 | 30th " | 1,183,671 | " | 17,483 | 63 |
| 1857 | 31st " | 1,115,654 | " | 17,986 | 36 |
| 1858 | 32d " | 1,075,323 | " | 17,378 | 15 |
| 1859 | 33d " | 1,016,931 | " | 17,109 | 96 |
| 1860 | 34th " | 1,200,051 | " | 17,227 | 92 |
| 1861 | 35th " | 1,013,783 | " | 17,202 | 79 |
| 1862 | 36th " | 1,112,264 | " | 18,100 | 00 |
| 1863 | 37th " | 1,006,901 | " | 21,855 | 01 |
| 1864 | 38th " | 1,112,264 | " | 26,477 | 59 |
| 1865 | 39th " | 1,006,901 | " | 29,064 | 23 |
| 1866 | 40th " | 1,076,779 | " | 36,108 | 42 |
| 1867 | 41st " | 1,007,881 | " | 44,691 | 79 |
| 1868 | 42d " | 1,310,756 | " | 46,245 | 18 |
| 1869 | 43d " | 1,175,000 | " | 53,188 | 26 |
| 1870 | 44th " | 1,151,394 | " | 50,556 | 86 |
| 1871 | 45th " | 1,000,539 | " | 51,030 | 77 |
| 1872 | 46th " | 848,259 | " | 48,622 | 99 |
| 1873 | 47th " | 802,136 | " | 42,687 | 28 |
| 1874 | 48th " | 669,176 | " | 42,687 | 28 |
| 1875 | 49th " | 675,000 | " | 39,669 | 96 |
| 1876 | 50th " | 750,000 | " | 37,819 | 11 |

Aggregating nearly fifty millions of copies of tracts—not pages; and over one million of dollars; an average of one million of tracts for every year, with an annual expenditure of $20,000 for missionary work.

## V.

## PLANS AND METHODS.

Pastors and laymen are continually calling upon us for information as to the means and instrumentalities we employ in carrying forward the work of city evangelization; and we cordially invite them to our missionary conferences, and throw open the doors of our office and our mission rooms and chapels, and give them every opportunity of a personal examination and study. In our reports and documents, and through the press in various ways, we are seeking to give the Christian public at large the results of our experience and observation.

In this line we now proceed to give some extracts from the recent report of a lay missionary, in which he presents a summary of his labors for fourteen years, believing that this inside view of the missionary work of a single laborer, for a series of years, will not be without encouragement to those engaged in similar operations, and will afford matter of interest to all. This missionary says that during this period of fourteen years he has given 364 Bibles to different families, and many of these have learned to love the word of God. He says of one:

"A Roman-catholic woman who had received a copy of the Bible hid it through the day, but when night came, and the board shutters of her casement windows were closed, her boy read to her out of the book that told her of the way of life, and she drank in of the precious truth with gladness. Another woman of the same faith, to whom I read Christ's sermon on the Mount sprang to her feet, and stopped me several times, exclaiming 'Oh how beautiful! how beautiful! I did not know that this was in the Bible.' 368 Testaments have been given, mostly to children attending Sabbath-school who had no Testaments of their own from which to learn their lessons. I have purchased from time to time, as occasion required, with my own means, such cheap religious books as I thought would be useful, and I find I have given away 242 of such volumes. I can trace several conversions to the reading of these precious books. One of the annual subscribers to the City Mission, who is a worthy member and an officer in one of the churches, was thus led to Christ. 1,257 children have been gathered into Sabbath-schools. Some of these were brought in by paid help, employed by the missionary to canvass certain localities which he was not able to do himself. A number of these children have grown up and become members of Protestant churches. Others are in places of trust and profit, good and upright citizens. Others, still, are teaching in Mission Sabbath-schools, where there are scholars. 376 children have been persuaded to go to the public day-schools, and some of these are now teachers in the schools where they were first placed as pupils. 184 young persons have been induced to join Bible classes, and of these some are now preaching the gospel of Christ. 660 persons have been persuaded to attend church. One of this number said :

"'I have not been to church in twenty-two years.' Another said : 'Mr.——, you are the first man that ever prayed in my family.' 130 temperance pledges have been obtained. Some very intemperate persons, nearly ruined, have been saved from the vice of drunkenness, and brought to true repentance and faith in Christ. As I am only a layman I have held no preaching services, distinctively so called, but I have conducted 1,413 prayer-meetings, in various tenement houses, in eleven different localities, and I cannot now think of any one meeting-place in which there were not some souls saved. In one house a meeting was held weekly for five years, in the room of a sick woman, who has recovered her health and been baptized into the spirit of our city missionary work. Fifty-six backsliders have been reclaimed. The most of these came from the Old World. They were members of churches in good standing at home. Families emigrated, part at a time, and those who came first left the Bible and religious books with those who remained behind. Here, among strangers, and not at once seeking a home in some church, they were gradually drawn into worldliness, and at length were found with the pleasure-seeking and Sabbath-breaking crowd. The city missionary going from house to house finds these wandering sheep, and by love and kindness wins them back to the Good Shepherd. I have made 42,000 visits to the widow and fatherless, the poor, the rich, and the dying; and it cheers me beyond expression to think how many persons in these visits I have had an opportunity of pointing to Jesus; and how many, from their cold garret and damp cellar-homes, looked away to the Saviour of sinners, and to the mansions and crowns and white robes reserved for those who are faithful unto death. In these missionary visits I have been cordially received, with very few exceptions. Even the Romanist has listened attentively while I have talked to him about the only Saviour, the only Mediator between God and man. And when I have prayed with him, he has asked God to bless me, and has said, 'You are the only man that ever prayed with me.' A scene occurred during one of these missionary visits I shall never forget. After praying with a poor sick Roman-catholic woman, she said: 'My priest never visited me but once, and then he went away angry because I had sent for him when I had no money to pay him, and he said he would never come again.' I cannot tell with what delight, and with what faith and hope, too, I pointed that poor, ignorant, dying woman to Jesus, the great High Priest who always cares when helpless sinners call, and who forgives without money and without price. She lived a few days after this, and left her dying charge with a neighbor in these words: 'Tell the man who prayed for me that I die, trusting in the great High Priest, who forgives sins without money.' This was pay enough for a life of missionary toil. 213 hopeful converts have united with Evangelical churches, and I have good reason to believe that many more, through our instrumentality, have been led to Jesus. Some persons, during their last illness, have given credible evidence of conversion, though we do not include such cases in our statistics. I remember an instance of hopeful conversion on a sick-bed; a sick man had long been visited, and constantly directed to Jesus as his only Saviour, till he felt the comforting influence of the Holy Spirit bearing witness of his acceptance. Then came a priest, and told him he was dying, and that he would go directly to hell, if he did not allow the offices of the church to be performed. The sick man said: 'I will risk it: I cannot sink. I feel the everlasting arms beneath me. Jesus saves me.'

"During the single year just passed—and this is a specimen of many of these fourteen years I have been reviewing—110 families have been aided, and $244 have been expended in their assistance. The principal part of this money has been put into my hands by a gentleman and his wife for this purpose. While preparing this report I have been twice to the attic home of a worthy American widow, who was very comfortably off during her husband's lifetime. Since then she has struggled to support herself and four little ones by making pants for 37½ cents a pair. I carried her what money she lacked of the rent and a basket of provisions. She said, 'I am afraid I cannot feed and clothe my children and pay the rent any longer; I shall have to put the three elder children into the Half-Orphan

Asylum.' This is the class of persons we aid, and this is the way in which we try to help them along. The amount of money given to any one family has been small, but it has been accompanied by a personal visit, when sad hearts have been met by sympathy and kindness, and they have been led to think of the Father in heaven, and have been taught and encouraged to pray as well as labor for their daily bread."

Thus far the report of our faithful, laborious missionary. Now let us add, that the City Mission has, on its records, the results of one thousand years of such missionary labor. That out of the investigations and observations of these humble visitors of the poor, have grown many of the most valuable and beneficial charities and reforms. The work, begun with a single man, forty-five years ago, has gone on, constantly increasing in numbers and influence. Now there are as many as 266 city missionaries in connection with the various missions and churches, who make 800,000 visits a year. And there are 118 mission schools and chapels, whose preaching and other religious and moral services, for adults or children, or both, are regularly carried on. And there are 300 religious, moral, and charitable societies and institutions.

The work of city evangelization, multifarious as it may be in its aspects, and special in its local adaptation, is yet a unit in design, one and the same everywhere and always, to bring sinners to Jesus.

Our plans may be briefly summed up in these few lines. The city missionary canvasses a given district; ascertains its available points; finds out the accessible families; wins his way by kindness and tact; establishes a prayer-meeting. The Holy Spirit owns the effort. Souls are converted. These bring in others. The place becomes too strait. A mission chapel is called for. Some of the Lord's stewards make an offering to the Lord for his love to them, and soon the mission building is reared and dedicated to Jesus for his glory, and given to the people for their Sabbath home. A minister is appointed, and the Christian ordinances are administered, and the converts bound together in a brotherhood of love. And now the same work of searching out, and bringing in, and saving, goes on as at the beginning. The poor are always moving. The tenement houses are always changing, and yet always full. The ranks of the poor and unfortunate are refilled every day. And the city missionary's work is never done.

## VI.

## A MISSIONARY REPORT.

"On a dark, cold winter night, a man was found leaning against a tree on the Battery, sobbing aloud. On inquiry, it was found that on the morning of that day—for it was the Sabbath—he had been to our mission, and there, by the Holy Spirit, through the truth preached, he was convicted of sin. Such was the distress of his mind, that he was obliged to leave his boardinghouse to seek a place to weep and pray. It appeared that the sermon brought to his mind the teachings of his godly mother, and the remembrance of the past broke his heart. The missionary gave such counsel and sympathy as were needed. Soon after the man left for Boston, and a letter since received announces that he has united with the church.

"A man from Rhode Island, who had been separated from his family two years by his intemperate habits, became so deeply impressed at the mission, that he returned to his boardinghouse and sought the Lord on his knees until two o'clock the next morning, when God spoke peace to his soul.

"A profane, intemperate German was persuaded

to attend the mission meeting. He was brought under conviction. A Testament and tracts were given him. And by these united means he was converted, and is now useful in the Lord's vineyard.

"A sick woman said, 'Two years ago I was in your chapel, and there I was led to see myself a sinner. I did as I was told to do. I went to Jesus, and I found in him all that my soul needed. Eighteen months ago I united with the church. I am not afraid to die.' The next day she went to be with Jesus, whom she loved.

"An immigrant on his way to P., stopping in at our mission, was seriously impressed by reading one of the placard hymns on the walls of the mission, and the words, 'Don't reject him!' went as an arrow to his heart. He felt he was guilty of rejecting Christ. He rose for prayer, determined not to live so any longer. Two days after he called to tell of his new-found hope in Christ.

"Visiting a boardinghouse, two men were seen, who said, 'One year ago, as we were passing through the city, we attended your mission. We were there convicted of our sin, and this was followed by converting grace. We are now members of the church in the place where we reside. We have come to

New York to meet friends expected from England.'

"A Romanist, who has lately united with a Protestant church, said, 'Before coming to the mission I worshipped God through saints and angels; but now I have Christ as my Priest and Mediator.' Another Romanist, while prayer was offered on his behalf, found peace to his soul."

And so the work goes on. We go from house to house, compelling the people to come in to our mission. We gather the children into our mission Sabbath-schools. We have the preaching of the gospel twice every Sabbath. We have our prayer-meetings through the week. We scatter tracts everywhere. And God blesses our work. To him be all the glory.

## VII.

### WHAT IT COSTS.

"It costs more than it will come to," used to be the fatal objection with the thoughtful and prudent. In most human affairs the outgoes and incomes may be calculated with remarkable certainty. In spiritual matters as well, there is a basis of calculation, only the result is not always directly within reach of ordinary human estimate.

Here are eight years and $4,000 expended in educating a young man for the ministry. What the returns will be we may safely estimate from well-ascertained facts. Here are $300,000 laid out in erecting a church, and the probable results scarcely leave room for conjecture in the presence of reliable data. Just now, in a well-considered paragraph in a religious newspaper, my eye caught these lines: "It costs more per man to make a Christian in London or in New York than it costs in heathendom." My first thought was, Well, what if it does? Does it cost more than it comes to? I can think of some of our mission converts, now preaching the Gospel in various places, the cost of whose conversion does not raise a question as to its economy. But then, looking into the reports of two Foreign Missionary organizations, I find that it costs $500 to $1,000 to make a Christian in heathendom, as the phrase is.

The records of the City Mission show that in fifty years the total expenditure has been $1,000,000, or $20,000 per year, and that, for the same period, the hopeful conversions have been 25,000, or 500 per year. If you divide $1,000,000 by 25,000 you will have $40, as the average cost of a convert.

## VIII.

## *PERSONAL EFFORT.*

The city missionaries are constantly laboring to promote the cause of temperance on Christian principles. Impelled by love, and armed with truth, they go from day to day among the homes of the poor, and in every way that Christian ingenuity can devise seek to save man from the evils of intemperance.

One of these faithful men, a little while ago, was laid up a few days with illness. One evening while he was confined to his bed, the door-bell rang, and the call being answered, it was found that a man had come, bringing a rose-bush in full-bloom to give to the missionary as a token of his grateful regard for what had been done for him. And what had been done for him? Simply this, and nothing more: the missionary had found the man, with a wife and two little children, in the depths of poverty and degradation, and all through the intemperate habits of the husband and father. The missionary visited the family frequently, and manifested a true Christian sympathy, and won the man's confidence and respect, so that he listened respectfully to his counsel and advice. He accompanied the missionary to the temperance meeting, and there voluntarily signed the pledge, and resolutely turned his back on his old companions and his evil ways. He has found business again, and is supporting his family, and promises well.

This incident is only given as an illustration of the hand-to-hand and heart-to-heart work of the City Mission. It is by personal effort for individuals that souls are saved. We do not know how to save masses. But every day shows us how men are saved. The returns of the City Mission for the last month give us ninety temperance pledges obtained, and twenty-nine hopeful conversions. This may seem to some like slow work, but it is sure. And the extension of this work is only limited by the men and the means. Given a sufficient number of faithful missionaries and an adequate supply of means, and the results would be multiplied accordingly.

## IX.

### FRUITFULNESS OF FRUIT.

It is only philosophical that when one sick man has been cured, he should tell his neighbor of his physician and the remedy. And it is perfectly natural that a soul who has found the balm of Gilead, and the good physician there, should publish abroad what grace has done, and persuade others to try the same. The records of City Missions furnish many illustrations in point. A man living far from God, who had not been to church in twenty years, is brought under the influence of the truth; he finds in the chapel practical sympathy and kind consideration and pleasant society, and becoming a new man in Christ Jesus, he at once goes after his neighbor, and brings him to the place of prayer. And, now and then, these converts become missionaries and evangelists and preachers of the gospel, and are made instrumental in leading scores and hundreds to Christ. So the fruit of Christian effort for souls goes on, endlessly multiplying itself to all eternity.

A poor Swede came into a chapel, and was there taken by a brotherly hand and made to feel at home. He soon was found among the seekers and inquirers, and was led along by degrees until he emerged into the light and liberty of the gospel. He became an ardent student in the school of Christ, and advanced rapidly in grace and knowledge. The good pastor of the chapel, discovering in his convert unmistakable signs of promise, encouraged and aided his progress, and soon he was in a course of preparation for the ministry, and at length was duly ordained to preach the gospel. Returning to his native country with a burning zeal for souls, he soon was enabled to kindle a sacred enthusiasm among his people, which led to gracious spiritual revivals, and the establishment of a training-school and theological seminary in Stockholm, Sweden, which is sending out qualified teachers of the truth every year.

The annual report of the City Mission for 1859 makes mention of the fact, that four years before, or in 1855, the City Missionary laboring among the Jews discovered a poor, friendless Jew, and took him to his home and befriended him. Subsequently this man was led to embrace the truth as it is in Jesus, and commenced a course of study, with the purpose of entering upon the ministry of the gospel, and in 1859 he was sent forth by the church with which he was connected as a missionary to China. His linguistic knowledge and studious habits led the missionary brethren on the ground to commit to his hand the work of translation, and for several years he has been engaged in the same. How he has performed the part assigned him may be judged of in the following extract from a report on the subject: "The Old Testament has been translated by him out of the original Hebrew into a language understood by a population four times as large as in all the United States. This work, of itself, is one of the grandest monuments which the human mind has ever erected, and it is one of the noblest trophies of missionary zeal and learning."

This man, whose learning and diligence are so conspicuous in making the Mandarin Bible, has been consecrated a missionary bishop to China; and this is the man who in 1855 was led to Christ by a City Missionary. And so the City Mission has been the agent in giving missionaries to Sweden and China. Who can measure the far-reaching results of Christian effort for souls? How truly the poet has said:

"The good begun by thee, shall onward flow,
In many a branching stream, and wider grow."

## X.

### HOPE FOR DRUNKARDS.

As much interest is everywhere felt in the reformation of drunkards, and in the operation of the asylums and homes established therefor, an extract of a letter just received from the Rev. J.

Willett, the excellent and efficient superintendent of the Inebriates' Home for Kings county, is well worth attention. After briefly referring to the success and the failures, the lights and the shadows, the usual history of such work, Mr. Willett says:

"I set out with my work, believing that the grace of God, which saved a wretch like me, knows no limits, and can reach the vilest sinner in the universe. Some of our patients have come and gone once, twice, and almost a dozen times to and from the Home, and when everybody seemed to have given them up in despair, the Saviour has put his hand upon them and caused them to sing, 'Oh to grace how great a debtor.'

"But God usually works by means. We have to do with those whose system is diseased and poisoned by rum. There needs a physical regeneration, and in many cases, especially when the brain is damaged and the will power has received a shock, long restraint is essential to cure and reformation. Mere temporary expedients no doubt assuage a deal of present misery, but after all they seem only to bridge over the dangerous gulf from one debauch to another, without effecting much permanent good. But oh if Christian men and women would only make one united effort to close the dramshops, nine-tenths of the drunkards of the land would disappear.

"It is true that for a generation there would be the old topers to care for, and restrain, but the rising generation would be saved from this drink curse.

"It has been clearly demonstrated, by carefully-collected statistics, that pauperism and crime are governed by the number of drinking-places in any given city, as compared with the population, and that, too, independent of all provisions which may be made for the education and religious training of the inhabitants.

"When I was laboring as a City Missionary, I was sometimes distressed beyond measure at the thought that any one of the almost numberless rum-shops in my district was destroying more souls than I was made instrumental in saving."

With this full understanding of all the difficulties of the situation, this faithful man, in the spirit of the divine Master, perseveres in his arduous undertaking, and is permitted to see the fruit of his labor. In the Inebriates' Home for Kings county, pleasantly situated on the bay, near Fort Hamilton, there were treated last year 152 males and 87 females. Total 239. Of the patients whose history can be traced, about one-fourth are known to be doing well. Others are improved, several are dead, and about one-third may be regarded as incurable cases.

It should be known that this is the only institution of the kind in this state that admits female patients of the better class, and for these special accommodations are provided. Paying patients will be received from any part of the country. Free patients are only received, except in special cases, from Kings county.

And it should be known to the City Missionaries and laborers among the poor in New York, that there is an Inebriates' Home on Ward's Island, under the management of the Commissioners of Charities. Application for admission thereto, should be made at the office, No. 66 Third avenue. Patients who are willing and able to labor, will be admitted without charge, when they will be required to work for their living. Others pay from $3 to $25 per week for board, as may be agreed upon, and are not expected to labor.

Homes for the care and cure of drunkards are being opened in Boston, Philadelphia, and in other cities, and much is being accomplished. At our Carmel Chapel in the Bowery, and at the Helping

Hand in Water street, and indeed, we may say, at all the missions stations, the faithful City Missionaries are using their utmost efforts to rescue men from the evils of intemperance. Let all good men pray for, and help on, these earnest self-denying laborers.

## XI.

### TRACT WORK.

In the great revivals of 1830-5, tract visitors were conspicuously useful in inviting people to church, and in following them with prayer and effort.

In 1836, Rev. Dr. E. F. Hatfield, then pastor of the Seventh Presbyterian Church, reviewing the labors of the previous season, wrote of these useful operations as follows: "On the first Sabbath of February last I gave notice that our house of worship would be opened every evening in the week for divine service; at the same time I requested the tract visitors to take the opportunity on the following day to distribute the monthly tract, and invite every family in their several districts to attend the meetings, or if they had already distributed the tract, to make a special visit for the purpose of persuading all to attend. In the course of the two or three following days, I have reason to believe that almost every family in the ward that was accessible, and not connected with some other denomination, had thus received notice of the meetings, and been urged to attend. It pleased the Lord wonderfully to manifest his power at that season in saving souls by the preaching of the word. Not less than four hundred souls were converted to God, of whom about three hundred connected themselves with my church. Of those thus received, the great majority were heads of families, and very many of them strangers, persons who had only occasionally been seen in our church, and some of them scarcely once or twice a year. I have every reason to believe that many of them were induced to come by the urgency of the tract visitor, and many of them declared that such was the case; indeed, during the whole month, these visitors, seventy or eighty in number, were abundant in labors."

And in all the subsequent history of evangelistic movements, the same general plan of operations has been prosecuted. The formation of new associations, and the adoption of new methods, have somewhat modified the old ways of working, yet all Christian workers are led, sooner or later, to feel that it is personal effort—which is only another name for tract effort—that, after all, is to be relied upon as the most effective agency for bringing souls to Christ.

The pastor of one of our city mission churches, in a recent report, says: "The spiritual influences abroad in the land have visited us with their blessings, awakening a new interest in the things of Christ's kingdom. Our meetings have been exceptionally well attended, and those for social prayer and conference have been more generally participated in. Many who never before have taken any part, have heartily spoken for Jesus, and to edification, and there has also been apparent a general earnestness in seeking the salvation of souls. In the matter of volunteer tract distribution, a new impulse has been imparted, so that the number engaged in this work has more than doubled during the past two months. All my experience in this work among the poorer classes encourages me in my labor, and I greatly esteem and value the zeal and coöperation of my faithful tract visitors."

## XII.

### HOW TO HELP THE POOR.

The city missionary is charged with the care of souls, and his first duty is to spread the good tidings of the gospel feast; and wherever he goes among the poor and sick and afflicted and distressed, he desires to be known as a Christian teacher, making known the truth as it is in Jesus. With good judgment and ready tact he deals wisely with the applications made for temporal relief, and applies such means as are committed to his hands for distribution in such ways as will not only not hinder his more spiritual work, but will the rather more surely promote his success in the main business of dealing with souls.

The past winter season has been exceptionally trying, in that cases of great physical suffering have abounded, and the means of affording relief have been seriously restricted, and the city missionary, as a burden-bearer, has been nearly overwhelmed with the sins and the sorrows he could not alleviate. How the city missionary labors at his spiritual work, and affords occasional relief to the poor without pauperizing them, may be seen in the following extract from a recent report: "I found the wife of a man, once in prosperous circumstances, now living in an obscure basement. She was sick, which gave me the opportunity to proffer some needed delicacies, and the kindness so won upon the woman's confidence that she frankly told me of her husband's struggles, how hard they had struggled to keep up and conceal from their neighbors their real condition of want. It was a pleasure to minister to the necessity of those who would have suffered long in silence rather than make known the want which was pressing both her and her husband to the direst extremity. I had a very frank and candid conversation with the sick woman in reference to the claims of religion, and she knew and acknowledged them, and professed her desire to become a Christian, and yet in a cautious way, that showed she did not wish to commit herself to the extent of promising what she did not in her heart feel determined to fulfil. My visits have been repeated, and after awhile I ascertained that once she had hoped in Christ and had intended to join the church, but for some reason had delayed the duty. Now she is evidently concerned about her neglect and anxious to take a stand for Christ, and is looking forward with pleasure to the time when she will be publicly received into church fellowship.

"A year ago I had become interested in a man who promised well, aided him in securing employment, and thought he was getting along nicely, when he fell to drinking and soon lost his place, and neglected his family and disappointed all my hopes. During the season just past I had met this man a number of times, and on one or two occasions he had told me how hard he was struggling to get bread for his family, but had not asked me for aid, probably because of his consciousness of having abused the confidence I had reposed in him the previous winter. However, I met him again one day, and walked with him some distance, and had a very plain talk with him, telling him how much we had been disappointed in him in the experience of the former winter. He confessed all, and more than all I had reproached him with, but said he had bitterly repented his misconduct, and was resolved never to taste liquor again. He appeared so humble and sincere, I accepted his confessions, and engaged to give him needed encouragement and help. He attended a prayer-meeting, and was strengthened in his good resolutions, and voluntarily signed the temperance pledge, and gives every indication of his determination to persevere. He frequently calls and expresses his gratitude for the good counsel given him, and speaks of his wonderful change, as he calls it. He feels as if he were in a new world. The prayer-meeting is his delight, the Bible is his daily guide, and he seems to be travelling in the paths of pleasantness and peace. He is supporting his family, and will soon be able to help others in distress. And this is the way that city missionaries aid the poor—helping them to help themselves; and not only this, but showing them how to help others also. Self-help is the best help for the poor, and the soul of charity is charity for the soul."

## XIII.

### WHAT CAN I DO?

THE question recurs, "What can I do?" Much will depend on your age, sex, condition, advantages, the number and the kind of talents God has put into your hand. You must consider these, and lay out your capital to the best advantage. Let us mention some fields, and you can consider if there be any one of them you could cultivate.

Your own family. Are all its members godly?

Have they all a place in the church? No? Then you have a work at your door. Pray, reflect; look for the side on which you can bring help. There is a child not receiving any teaching. There is a want of religious reading even for Sabbaths. The child could be got to Sabbath-school. A good serial could be got to tempt the careless to read. There is no regular attendance at church, no seat in a church perhaps. Could you manage to get this arranged? There are servants in the house? Are they Christians? Or do you know anything about them? Inquiry even might do good. Try all ways at home. A light is brightest to those who are closest to it.

Your relatives—how is it with them? Are they Christians? All? Some are not, not even being approached. Can you approach them with affection, gentleness, at the right time, and in the right way? Do you live so that they will respect you and attach weight to what you say? Do you carry yourself so that they will love you? You are the very person of all others, perhaps, to bring the truth to a cousin, an aunt, a nephew. Remember how Joseph provided bread for his brethren and their households, ill as they treated him.

Who lives next door? Are those neighbors to

whom you bow on the steps Christians? Have they a pastor? Do the children learn saving truth? When they are sick, do you show them the gentle side of Christianity—that which it turns to the suffering? Do you offer any comfort in sorrow? They know you to be a Christian, perhaps. They must wonder that you have no care for their souls. Perhaps they think your religion is only a form. You will be and they will be at the judgment-day. What will there be to look back on of effort made for them?

In what congregation do you worship? Is the minister ever cast down? Are all the committees full and in good spirits? Is there any part of the work falling behind? Could you help it on? You have some place already. Do you fill it effectively? Do you really "take hold"? Are you doing your work with your might?

There are various "societies" around you. They find it hard to get working members of boards and committees. You would be amazed to learn how hard it is for some of them to get a quorum at meetings for business. They have "honorary members" and ornamental members, nominal members and contributing members, who give money and nothing else; and secretaries have great trouble to contrive for the faithful doing of the business. Could you aid? Do you help with your means? To be sure, the societies are not all perfect; but they all do some and many of them much good that might not be done otherwise.

"Who are with you in the office?" Other young men do not fail to tell of the theatres, entertainments, and "sights" they enjoy. You have heard of their pleasures. Do you tell them with equal enthusiasm of yours? They tell of their "good times," advertise their haunts, and commend their entertainers. Do you?

But you are a lady. Well, how are the poor neighbors around you? Are there any girls likely to grow up without knowing the use of a needle? Sewing-schools, free, once a week, taught by ladies, and their toils with scissors and stitches relieved by a pleasant hymn and a Scripture verse, and consecrated by a prayer—which perhaps the poor little girls never joined in at home—such have done great good.

Are there any rough boys around you, growing up in godlessness, getting ready for the penitentiary? A Christian lady is just the person to do some of them good. Her sex wins deference, except from the worst; and her gentleness softens them. Are there any poor, overworked mothers near you, to whom life is perpetual, unrelieved toil? "Mothers' meetings" have done them good. They need not be large; indeed a small meeting is often best, for you can get near their burdened hearts. They cannot go to church, or get dressed, or get their clothes settled, "for the children." There is a way of carrying the church and the truth and all Christian charities to them.

Are there any near you, accessible to you, clearly going to ruin? There is your neighbor's son learning to drink. You saw him reeling the other evening. "Run, speak to that young man." A timely word may save him. The woman who waits on you is becoming entangled in a bad association. She is your sister—fond of you, perhaps—will you let her go unwarned?

"Ah, but," you say, "it is so hard to do these things; it requires a sacrifice." Just so. The Lord knows that. He says so: "With such sacrifices God is well pleased."     Rev. Dr. Hall.

## XIV.

### *THE SOUL THAT STANDS NEXT TO YOU.*

It is disheartening to find now-a-days so many people on a strain. Everybody seems determined to do a big thing or nothing. One wants a fresh field ; one wants more scope ; another wants to try a new instrument. Whereas the field that is nearest is the best for anybody. Think of this vast world of ruin and sin all around us, actually touching us at every point. How it welcomes even the least help which is honestly offered to it! Did you ever lay your finger upon the edge of a bird's nest, when the mother was absent, and mark how blindly, but instinctively, those callow necks and open bills all stretched up towards you for food? So the whole human race stands expectant. If you have any good to offer, it is folly to talk about a fresh field. There are a million hearts all round you that need it. And your earliest office is to aid the soul that stands next to you.

Then as to more scope, it is enough to say that any one who is really in earnest can find all the organizations, all the appliances, all the helps he can possibly employ. I do not believe in those people who think, or assert, that the ordinary churches to which we all belong are Laodicean, or that they fail of their end. I have no confidence in such persons who grow busy in framing associations and organizing societies, but never get to work in real service. I feel anxious about the souls that stand next to them. I was struck with the wit and wisdom of a reply I once overheard. One of my ministerial brethren, of rare common sense, was asked what he thought about these new-fangled sisterhoods, proposed in certain quarters. He answered, "I think very well of the sisters, but I cannot say I admire the hoods."

Also as to the instruments, one word of deprecation is needed. Our Sunday-school conventions are full of models as the Patent-office is full of patterns. Even in grace I readily admit there may be economy of spiritual force in a measurable use of labor-saving machines. But one may learn a lesson from the satire of even Gulliver's Travels. The tailor in Laputa took the measure of his customers for a suit of clothes by trigonometry; and yet it is not recorded that he escaped danger of a misfit. We may exhaust much valuable energy in mere friction of apparatus. And that is a most unhealthy movement, when it is discovered that helps have become hindrances. That is to say, every subterfuge which occupies time and diverts attention to itself, so as to turn any Christian's effort away from commonplace personal work, and the quiet use of the Scriptural means, every excuse found in the unwelcomeness of the field, every delay forced by the search after a fresh way of doing things, is suspicious. Human endeavor will find spiritual reward best in laboring for the soul that stands next to us.

Rev. C. S. Robinson, D. D.

---

## XV.

### DOING ONE'S DUTY.

Of one period of this old earth's history it stands recorded, "There were giants in those days." This certainly was before our time. The age we live in is not altogether heroic. But now and then there are stories in the papers of souls who die for right and die for duty. It flashes out in unanticipated brilliancy, as a new truth, that fidelity to commonplace demands is a species of fine heroism. Thus some, whose lives or calling we deem homely, suddenly appear shining in the royal robes of a manhood unquestioned. A soldier, the father of a family, the senator of a state, puts his written order for an advance in his hatband, goes straight to what he knows is death, and in an hour lies silent with a bullet in his brain. An engineer sees a drawbridge open, and knows there is safety for those he bears in his train only by the sacrifice of his own life; one moment of decision ends it; and, face upwards in the stream, with the locomotive crushing his chest, the simple-minded hero goes out in the silence, while the saved passengers waken with the shock that plants them across. And just now there rises on our kindled imagination the form of that sea-captain who went quietly forward, as the ship kept sinking, lifting the women over the side into boats, pistol in his hand, demanding obedience of the crew; then at last his wife, six months a bride, is led over the ladder, and from the tossing thwart looks back for her last upon the form of her brave husband, and pleads to go on the deck again and die with him. The night is dark in the Channel, but no star ever glittered in gloom so brightly as that fine figure of manhood glistens in our remembrance when we think of him faithful to the end. Somehow we feel constrained to identify ourselves with such people. If there can be any funeral, we are bound to be there. We walk in the procession. We reverently lay hold of one corner of the pall. A common brotherhood claims us. Nor does the impression end in mere pitiful admiration. For all time thereafter, wherever the language is spoken, the pure become purer, the brave become braver, the manly become manlier. We straighten up to more height, like proud children, when our parents' names are repeated with praise. We walk with foreheads cleared of clouds, and actually begin to believe in men.

In our times we have very little conception of what is meant by martyrdom of that savage and extreme kind which Stephen endured. Men established Christianity by dying for its confirmation. They are enabled now to commend it better by living for its spread. It is, therefore, not an ambition for us to cherish, even with high heroics, in these quieter days, when piety kept decorously has grown respectable, to advance to the edge of the precipice singing, and under the hail of stones dashing life into atoms, seek the presence of the blessed. Our privilege ought to be the dearer because it is really the more difficult to glorify God in some tame and commonplace way. Thus it comes to pass that holy living and brave dying are most intimately connected. There are modest men and gentle women, all over this Christian world of ours, who day by day do duty as finely as ever Stephen did, and who, when the last day comes, peacefully make ready to die with all of his triumph, and yet none of his show. Indeed, few raptures of the deathbed are ever striking enough to be put into print. Most lamps go out quietly as the oil fails. And in the majority of instances it comes to pass that we have to ponder the sweet, dear record of unobtrusive excellence some little time before we fairly see that a great life has entered the shadows and is gone. He can hardly be considered a manly man who does not wish for this posthumous tribute of affectionate remembrance. How simple and bare are such words as these, perhaps spoken by some pall-bearers, "devout men," at our funeral: "He was a faithful man, and did his duty." Yet it seems as if they would make the cold face and heart stir in the coffin! Oh, the beauty and glory of one's being dead, and yet speaking, so that what is honest and true and pure and gentle and Christlike is helped and encouraged.   Rev. C. S. Robinson, D. D.

## XVI.

### *TAKE A STAND.*

When Daniel went to Babylon, he took his stand; the meat and the wine which were offered him he refused to eat. He knew that the wine had been offered up to idols, and he refused to partake of what had been thus polluted. He saw that the law of God and the law of the great king Nebuchadnezzar were in conflict, but he obeyed the law of God. He was a man of faith and of belief. In ten days he looked healthier than any of those who ate as the king had ordered. He had taken his stand for God, and God blessed him. Young man, you that have just come to New York, is there not a lesson in this story for you? Does your employer ask you to work on Sunday? Take your stand. If God's law conflicts with man's, adhere to the living God. He will help you. You may have promised that loving, praying mother of yours that you would not go to the theatre. Are you tempted to go? Does some friend invite you and urge you to go with him? Take your stand. Learn to say No. Yield with no compromise. It is this miserable, compromising spirit that ruins so many. Supposing we, of these times, had been in Babylon when Daniel was tempted. Why, we'd have advised something like this: "Now, Daniel, you know you are not in Jerusalem. You're a poor heathen captive" —now here's the advice of the Christianity of the nineteenth century—"you're in Babylon, Daniel, and do as the people of Babylon do. You know wine is better than water, and water wont agree with you. The water of the Euphrates will make you sick. We know that the wine has been offered to idols, but God will wink at it if you drink while you are down here." But, thank God, that man took his stand, and kept his faith.

The king had a dream, and Daniel said, "I'll tell the king's dream, only give me time." Ah, see what faith he had. He knew that God would keep him right. And that night he prayed long and faithfully that God would reveal the secret. He went to sleep and had a dream, in which God revealed the secret. He arose and went to the king and was asked if he could tell the dream. Daniel, with the same faith in God, said that his God was able; he gave God all the glory. He told the king what he had dreamed, how his Chaldean kingdom would be overthrown and divided, how Greeks and Romans and others would overrun it and divide its possessions. "That's my dream," said Nebuchadnezzar; and an edict went forth, making Daniel a ruler among the mighty. But another trial came. The king ordered his image to be set up on the plains. There are three men there who will not bow down to it. They are Shadrach, Meshach, and Abed-nego. And the king is very angry, and orders the furnace to be heated seven times hotter. And when they came forth, with not so much as a hair of their heads burned, another edict went forth, that any man who said anything against the God of Shadrach should incur the wrath of the king. Young man, will you take your stand as these men did?

D. L. Moody.

## XVII.

### DANGER OF NEGLECTING ONE CHILD.

A REMARKABLE case of criminal inheritance has been traced back during the past year by the New York Prison Association, showing the overwhelming importance to the community of caring for even two or three vagrant children.

About one hundred years ago, there lived on the borders of two or three forest lakes in Ulster county, New York, a little vagrant girl called "Margaret, and four sisters, some of whom were of illegitimate birth. They seem to have been in no respect different from hundreds of little girls in and around this city who yearly come under the care of this Society. Their parents were poor, roving people, who made their living partly by hunting and fishing, and partly by stealing. They lived, like our poor city children, crowded in shanties, where old and young, male and female, slept in the same rooms. Like our street children, they never went to school or attended church. They grew up almost untouched by the morality and religion of the day. In the winter they were aided by the outdoor relief of the authorities, or by kind-hearted persons, and in the summer they lived on game and on their plunder from farms and barnyards. Probably as most people passed little Maragret, the future "mother of criminals," they looked on her as people do now on the little ragged street-sweepers they meet on our streets, either with utter indifference or with hopelessness, as on an irreclaimable vagabond, or with disgust, as one with whom the decent and virtuous should have nothing to do. The little Margaret grew up thus to a wicked womanhood.

In a recent visit to the Kingston jail, the able official of the Association, Mr. Dugdale, came upon the following criminals, all of whom he found to belong to the same family: the oldest, a man fifty-five years of age, awaiting trial for receiving stolen goods; his daughter, aged eighteen, (subsequently arrested as a prostitute,) held as a witness against him; her uncle, aged forty-two, for burglary in the first degree; the illegitimate daughter of the latter's wife, aged twelve years, upon which child he had attempted violence, and who was awaiting sentence for vagrancy, and two brothers, aged nineteen and fourteen, accused of an assault with intent to kill, they having pushed a child over a cliff forty feet high, and nearly killed him by the fall.

He traced back the genealogy of these criminals, and discovered that the ancestor of them all was the little vagrant girl of whom we have spoken, or her sisters. This stimulated his efforts, and after immense labor he finally brought to light the following striking facts as to this unhappy family:

Seven hundred and nine (709) descendants of Margaret and her sisters are accurately tabulated, whose names are mainly taken from public records. Of these 91 are known to be illegitimate, and 368 legitimate, leaving 250 unknown as to birth. One hundred and twenty-eight (128) are known to be prostitutes, 18 kept houses of bad repute, and 67 were diseased, and therefore cared for by the public. Only 22 ever acquired property, and eight of these lost what they had gained. One hundred and forty-two (142) received out-door relief during an aggregate number of 734 years, 64 were in the almshouse of the county, and spent there an aggregate number of 96 years; 76 were publicly recorded as criminals, having committed 115 offences, and been 116 years in jails and prisons.

The crimes of the females were licentiousness, and those of the males violence and theft. But the record we have quoted is merely their public history of criminality, which is necessarily very imperfect. Great numbers of the offences of this wretched family were never entered on any court records, and hundreds were never even brought to trial. It is well known that this young "mother of criminals" and her sisters have poured a stream of disease, licentiousness, insanity, idiocy, pauperism, and crime over the county now for a hundred years. This fearful current has not yet ceased to flow, as some of the descendants in the sixth generation survive in our own House of Refuge.

Fifty per cent. of all direct female descendants of Margaret became prostitutes, and of the whole stock, from the age of twelve upwards, fifty per cent. are found to be of disreputable character. Murder or attempts to murder appear among the males in every generation except the sixth, where the children are not older than seven years. Forgery is found but once on their records. Theft appears everywhere.

Another appalling feature in this history of criminal inheritance is the disease spread through the county by these vagrant children, and the consequent lunacy, idiocy, epilepsy, and final weakness of body and mind which belong to inherited pauperism, transmitted to so many human beings.

Mr. Dugdale has traced still farther the line, and makes it probable that the aggregate of the descendants of these vagrant children reach the large amount of 1,200 persons living and dead.

The cost of their almshouse relief he estimates as $15,000, and their out-door relief as $32,250 to Ulster county; the maintenance of the prisoners of this family at $100 per annum, as $14,000; the cost of arrest and trial at $100 for each case, at $25,000; the amount of property stolen or destroyed by them, at $15,000, and so on in various items, until he reaches the sum of $1,023,600 as the cost to Ulster county and the state of New York for neglecting one vagrant child and her miserable little sisters.

## XVIII.

### HOW TO SAVE SOULS.

Souls are saved through the agency of the truth; therefore, it is the duty of every one to endeavor to be familiar with the truth, by the study of the Bible and good books, and by strict, faithful, and prayerful attention to the preached word. Without familiarity with the truth, no Christian can become useful in the highest degree.

You can work for Christ—

By giving and lending tracts and good books.

By punctually meeting all your religious engagements.

By persevering efforts to bring acquaintances and strangers to the prayer-meetings and Sabbath services of the church, and by learning or teaching in the Sabbath-school.

By cultivating a spirit of sociability and Christian fellowship, especially among members of the church, and in the house of worship.

By visiting the sick, the poor, strangers and acquaintances, in the spirit of the Master.

By cordial attention to strangers.

By endeavoring to be familiar with the progress of the kingdom of heaven on earth, as indicated by the great Christian enterprise of the church, at home and abroad.

By giving, as God hath prospered you, punctually and regularly, for the current expenses of your church, and for the salvation of the world.

By earnest and regular secret prayer for the prosperity of your own church, and the whole church of Christ.

By testimony for Christ, many are awakened, and others edified. "Go home to thy friends, and tell them how great things the Lord hath done for thee."

By holding neighborhood prayer-meetings with the advice of pastor and elders. In this way great good is often done.

By direct personal appeals to the unconverted to come at once to Christ. Every Christian ought to win souls to the Saviour.

By studiously conforming to Christian principles in all business transactions.

## XIX.

### A MISSION CONVERT BECOMES A MISSIONARY.

FORTY years ago a family of English immigrants arrived in this city whose character and habits promised nothing but degradation and ruin for themselves, and harm and loss to the community. The father was a man of fair natural abilities, had seen something of the world, was a good mechanic, and capable of filling a respectable position in life, but he had given a loose rein to sensual appetites until the barriers of self-restraint were swept away and he and his sons alike had become intemperate, improvident, and reckless, and the place they called home was the abode of strife and confusion and every evil work.

This father and one of his sons, after much persuasion, were induced to attend a religious meeting which had been commenced in their neighborhood, especially for the benefit of those who were not reached by the ordinary means of grace. At the close of the meeting a few words were addressed to them alone, and they were urged to attend to the interests of their souls. The father said curtly: "If we are to be saved, we shall be; and if not, all that we can do will be of no avail," and walked away.

To the surprise of those who knew their natural stubbornness and prejudice, they appeared in the meeting again the next week, and when they were spoken to in a friendly way after the service, it appeared that the Holy Spirit had already brought them to some reflection, for now the reply was soberly given: "Either we are wise and you are fools, or we are fools and you are wise."

The following week found them again in the place of prayer, listening with evident interest to the simple presentation of the gospel. And now, when personally addressed, the reply came in the form of the inquiry: "Men and brethren, what must I do?" It was plain that the father, at least, had determined on a new course, and he was encouraged and aided in every way that Christian love could devise. Such had been his manner of life, and such the strength of evil habits and the pernicious influence of his bad example, that his way seemed beset with the most formidable difficulties; but he felt that every obstacle must be overcome, he must go forward or he must die; and casting himself upon the Lord, he was enabled to persevere.

After a few days he said to his family: "I can no longer sit down to partake of the bounties of a kind Father without asking his blessing." This opened the way for family worship, which he next instituted, and at the prayer-meeting soon after, he took part in the service, calling upon the name of the Lord, and with a broken and contrite spirit confessed his sins. In the language of a child he spoke of his wanderings, and of the way in which Providence had led him. He praised God for having brought him to this land, and placed him under such gracious influences. "Oh! who would have expected," he exclaimed, "to find such a worthless worm of the dust among the people of God?" He soon made an open profession of his faith in the Redeemer, and took his family to church and his children to Sabbath-school.

As might be expected, this great outward moral revolution was attended with, and followed by, the most marked change in the outward life and surroundings; the whole aspect of the family was altered for better, and their condition in every respect greatly improved. Having been furnished with a small capital, they were enabled to go on with their trade—work, more than they could accomplish, was offered them—all were busy, and all comparatively happy.

It may well be supposed that this man, saved through the faithful exertions of active Christians, would himself feel a peculiar interest in similar efforts; and soon he was seen engaged in going from house to house, as he could find time, speaking in plain honest phrase of a Saviour's love, and gathering people into the house of prayer; and not without effect, for the Holy Spirit owned and blessed these humble endeavors, and many were converted to God. And so he continued for years to labor with such marked consistency, prudence and skill, that his brethren felt that the Spirit had designated him for the work, and he was accordingly appointed as a missionary, and in this relation served his Master with great zeal and success for twenty years, when he went to his grave in a full age, like as a shock of corn cometh in, in his season.

## XX.

### SCANDINAVIANS.

AMONG the recent deaths has been that of a good man, known for thirty years as Pastor Hedstrom of the Bethel Ship, or Mission for Scandinavians, at Pier No. 11, North River. And this revives some recollections of the commencement of the missionary operations among that interesting people, which I will briefly narrate.

Some years prior to 1845, a young sea-captain, Roland Gelston, was converted, and at once commenced a life of Christian activity, as a tract visitor among seamen. In the prosecution of his labors, he visited sailors in the New York Hospital, laid a tract upon the breast of a sleeping Swedish sailor, who, upon awaking, read it, and resolved, if spared, to enter upon a new life. This man was Peter Bergner, who came to be connected with the Mariner's church, then in Roosevelt street, under the care of Rev. Henry Chase. Bergner was by trade a ship-carpenter, and while at his work would talk to such of his countrymen as he found, and persuade them to come to his house, where he would talk and pray with them. Meantime a ship, the Henry Leeds, had been purchased, dismantled, and fitted up as a church by the Wesleyan Methodists. These people attempted the maintenance of a mission to seamen, longshoremen, and others, and Bergner obtained permission to hold meetings also for his countrymen.

Bergner, working in the First ward, soon came under the notice of the city missionary of the ward, who at once brought the man and his work to the attention of his associates in the City Mission, and great interest was awakened in behalf of the Scandinavian population. Statistics were gathered, and a statement was prepared and laid before the Missionary Society of the Methodist Episcopal Church. At the same time the Bethel ship had been given up by the Wesleyan Methodists, and was for sale, and Mr. Hedstrom was within reach, so the Missionary Society made an appropriation, and the Methodist church authorities appointed Mr. Hedstrom as missionary to the Scandinavians, and he commenced his work in 1845, and with him Peter Bergner, as a true yokefellow, labored most faithfully for twenty years, or until his death, in 1866, being sustained in his work by the City Mission.

From this first evangelical missionary effort among the Scandinavians in this country has come the following statistical results, gathered from the last Annual Report of the Missionary Society of the Methodist Episcopal church. It appears that in Denmark, Sweden, and Norway together, there are 81 ministers, 87 churches and preaching places, and 8,409 communicants. And in the Scandinavian missions in this country there are 70 ministers, 70 churches, and 5,190 communicants. And beside this, other Protestant denominations have been equally active in instituting missions among the people, and show gratifying returns for their work. So a little seed has become a tree, according to the word of the Lord.

## THE COSMOPOLITAN CITY.

Hardly any city has a greater variety of population than New York. Not only are all the sections and states of the Union represented here, but most of the nations of the earth. The State Census of 1875 gives the number of persons born in Ireland as 199,084, and if we add to this for the children of Irish parentage born in this city, 100,000, we may estimate the Irish population at 300,000. From the same census we learn that the number of persons born in Germany is 165,021, and adding 85,000 to this for the children of German parents born in this city, we may suppose that the German population is not far from 250,000. Other nationalities are given as follows: Persons born in England, 26,913; in Scotland, 7,635; in Canada, 3,979. Then there are thousands of French, Italians, Spaniards, Cubans, and Portuguese, and numbers of Russians, Swedes, Finns, South-Americans, Norwegians, Mexicans, Greeks, Poles, Japanese, Bohemians, Chinese, East-Indians, with a few Armenians, Siamese, Hawaiians, Arabs, Copts, Malays, Thibetans, and Turks. Forty different languages are heard in our streets. Among all these people the city missionary goes, carrying the Scriptures and the tracts in their various tongues, and showing that friendly interest and Christian sympathy that needs no interpreter but the human heart.

## XXI.

### *LIVING AND TEACHING THE GOSPEL OF CHRIST.*

WHEN Christ had finished the work of laying the foundations of his kingdom in the world, in precisely what state did he leave it? He passed out of the view of men. He has never manifested himself to their gaze since. How much did he leave behind him? Moses wrote the law; Jesus Christ wrote nothing. The prophets wrote their prophecies; Jesus Christ wrote nothing. He lived, he spoke, he acted, he wrought, he died, he arose, he ascended into heaven. He left just simply the memory of what he was, and what he said, and what he did. It is a matter sometimes of amazement to thoughtful men, that our Lord did not leave from his own hand the portrait of himself, the record of his words, the history of his deeds. He left only a memory; but memory is the action of the mind, It must have existed then in the mind of men, and only there. It comes to this: Jesus

Christ left in the world a few men and women like-minded with himself, with whom was the same spirit which was also in Jesus. And that was all. Our Lord did not leave a long statement of the truth. He left men, women. If thereafter the truth was to be known, it must be known from them. If thereafter the truth must be proved, it must be proved in them and by them. If thereafter the truth was to be illustrated, it must be illustrated in their life and death. Our Lord might have turned to his few followers as hs ascended upon the clouds of heaven, and said, after the manner of an apostle who said to his pupils, "Ye are my epistles—ye are my gospel." Men and women, then, were to remember the person of Christ, to cherish his character, to recall his words and works, and then go about telling all he was, whatever they could remember of what he had said, so much as they could distinctly recall of what he had done. In that state, in such keeping to be continued and propagated by such instruments, our Lord left that kingdom which he came down from heaven to establish in the earth. This explains our whole relation to the kingdom of Christ, and our whole work for the kingdom of Christ. We are, first, to know Jesus; we are, second, to preach Jesus. Now let me distinguish between certain facts historical and biographical about Jesus and knowing Jesus himself. Very many of the Jews knew the events in the personal history of Jesus Christ. Very many of them had overheard his discourses. Very many of them had witnessed his miracles. Some of them had seen him die. Some were aware of his resurrection. Some had heard of his ascension. But they did not comprehend him. His disciples seem to have been let somewhat into the secret of his person, the principles of his character, and the power of his holiness. Take, for example, any Jew who among the throng of followers had witnessed the teaching and the working of Jesus, and compare his knowledge and appreciation of him with the knowledge and appreciation of that disciple whom Jesus loved. The one knew Jesus Christ by name and exterior life; the other knew him by nature and by the interior and divine life. And it seems to me that Jesus gave more gospel in simply living before his disciples than even He who spake as never man spake would have uttered in any language given to mortals, or brought down from immortals. And this seems to have been the larger part of the gospel of Christ. We have a few conversations recorded, but exceedingly short. We have a few instructions that seem to be parts of extended discourses, but they are exceedingly brief. What he was, was more than what he said. What he manifested was more than he could utter. What he did was gospel. And so he seems to have gathered the disciples around him that they might know him. He ate bread with them. He lay down to sleep with them. He went through all the common offices of the humblest life in its intensest simplicity in companionship with them. He spoke naturally as opportunity was afforded or occasion demanded. He answered questions, he resolved difficulties, he consoled griefs, he relieved troubles. What he did say seems rather to have been drawn out of him than offered spontaneously by him, and so we find his sayings all intermixed with history, and not set apart by themselves in separateness. I believe that the philosophy of the mission of Jesus is to be found in the fact, that he was the brightness of the Father's glory, the express image of his person. He was the Godhead embodied. To give gospel was to show himself. Beyond that, to be sure, he was to die for man's guilt, to be humbled in the dust of death that he might rise again for man's justification. And on the cross there is the gospel also, but the person dying there for sinners is again the gospel. So throughout, as a manifestation of the nature of God and as a fulfilment of the will of God, Jesus Christ, acting while he lived and dying when his life was lived through, was himself gospel. Rev. Joseph T. Duryea, D. D.

## XXII.

### *WATER STREET.*

TEN years ago a faithful and laborious city missionary, now entered into his rest, was stationed near the Five Points. Often his heart was stirred within him as he saw crowds of unfortunate and friendless men drifting past him; and wishing to do them good, he drew them into his mission room; and when they were hungry he fed them from his own table; and at night, instead of sending them to the police station for lodging, gave them a blanket and a place on the benches in the mission room. This practical philanthropy becoming known, two of our down-town merchants craved the privilege of furnishing the means necessary to carry on the good work, and have ever since contributed to it liberally. In process of time it became expedient to change the location of the mission station, and one of the leading Nassau street bankers having on his hands a house in Water street, which he had purchased to redeem from the rum-trade and the business of prostitution, offered the same to the City Mission for their benevolent purposes. Through the aid of members of the Executive Committee and their friends the premises were cleaned and furnished, and opened for a free reading-room for workingmen and for religious meetings. So much encouragement attended this effort that it was resolved to rebuild; and last fall a plain, substantial brick building was erected on the same ground, 316 Water street, and the place is now known as the "McAuley Water-street Mission," and meetings are held every evening of the week and twice on the Sabbath, and all are well attended.

Since the humble effort first commenced ten years ago at the Five Points, the work of reclaiming the wandering and saving the abandoned has been steadily gaining in public favor and confidence. The new and attractive rooms opened at 316 Water street are witness to the faith of Christian men that the gospel can lift up even from the dens and slums of the Fourth ward. And five years ago a similar enterprise was started in the

Bowery, near Grand street, reaching perhaps a little better class of men, younger in years generally, and not so far gone in sin; and three thousand men each year are reached and benefited in one way and another through this chapel and its useful adjuncts.

In all our city mission chapels gospel temperance meetings are regularly carried on, and those who sign the pledge are visited and encouraged and kindly looked after; and numbers of men give credible evidence of a radical change in heart and life, and are supporting themselves respectably. Any one can see the money value of these missionary operations that take men who are a burden and expense to society and transform them into useful, self-supporting citizens and taxpayers.

## XXIII.

### *THE MASSES.*

There is a great deal of irresponsible and reckless talk about what are of late years called "The Masses." Some people speak of curing the evils among the masses—as if they were all diseased. Some urge a reformation of the masses—as if they were all vicious. Some suggest that the social system be reconstructed from the very foundations— as if the masses were bricks or blocks, and would be improved by being laid over again. Philanthropists and politicians, divines and demagogues, are all declaiming about the masses.

Just in order to receive correct ideas upon this great subject, it is proper sometimes to venture in one's own behalf an analysis of a vast multitude of men, women, and children; such, for instance, as that our Saviour saw from the heights of Golan, when the people followed him around the shore of Tiberias. "And Jesus, when he came out, saw much people, and was moved with compassion toward them, because they were as sheep not having a shepherd." The crowd seemed just like one of those vagrant flocks he was accustomed to notice on the slopes of such grassy hills.

The significant part of Jesus' comment is found in the suggestion of what these people lacked, and not of what they had. It was the spectacle of a negative, and not of a positive. Let us get this clear. What is cold? The mere absence of heat. What is darkness? The mere absence of light. What is ignorance? Absence of knowledge. What is sickness? Absence of health. Is it always wicked to be chilly, or sightless, or unlearned, or ill? That depends upon circumstances. A negative may become so severe, however, as to be a fearful reflection. They used to make me laugh when I was a child, telling me of some sandbanks by the seashore which caved away and left the holes of the homeless swallows sticking straight out in the air. But I have seen a lack so extensive that it became a prominent protuberance in a life, nevertheless. As our Lord saw that throng, and marked their excited looks, their aimless hurry, he compared them to a flock unfolded, unprotected, and unled. They were sheep, not with anything, but without something; not with diseases, but without a shepherd. A shepherd is everything to sheep. Such a negative lack is a positive loss. It may suggest new thought concerning the masses, to contemplate what they miss, as well as what they manifest.

It would be a salutary exercise for any Christian to go where he can spend a meditative hour in full view of a vast city. There is something exceedingly impressive in that voluminous body of sound which rises upon the ear, listening carefully to it from some high position overlooking the scene. Remember that this solemn murmur, seeming so like the majestic roar of the sea, is not by any means the roll of inanimate water against rocks without nerves. It is all alive. It is made up of sighs and songs, words and wailings, shouts of laughter and groans of pain, friendly greetings and bitter explosions of wrath. All these are mingled together and wrought into the same substance, the pure and the foul alike. As we listen to it, it represents one great swell of emotion absolutely instinct with vitality. It is thoroughly human as you and I, when we speak or weep or pray, are human.

Rev. C. S. Robinson, D. D.

## XXIV.

### CO-OPERATION.

THE New York City Mission and Tract Society, established on the common faith of evangelical Protestant Christianity, and working on the plan of Christian union and coöperation, has always cultivated fraternal relations with all who were working in the same line, and often joins its labors with those of kindred societies to the great advantage of both. At the present time such organizations of mutual helpfulness exist between the City Mission and several societies, among which may be named the New York Bible Society, the Association for Improving the Condition of the Poor, the Children's Aid Society, the Young Men's Christian Association, the Five Points House of Industry, and the Home of the Friendless.

The public mind is sometimes exercised with the apparently excessive multiplication of charitable societies, and insists that all of kindred aims shall be united in one organization. How far this would be wise or practicable is left for others to determine. For those who are actively engaged in carrying on the societies, it remains that they should study to promote reciprocal action between the several charitable organizations, with a view to greater economy and efficiency in the administration of relief, the exposure of professional beggars, the prevention of pauperism and crime, and the moral elevation of the worthy, industrious poor. For the purpose of giving accurate information concerning the charitable work in operation in New York, the City Mission has for fifteen years been giving to the public, with the beginning of each year, a pamphlet of 150 pages, with descriptive lists of all the benevolent societies and institutions. And that this publication meets a felt necessity is shown in the number of applications which are constantly made for it from January to December. In gathering the facts and statistics for this volume, the Secretary personally visits every institution in the city and studies the history of each.

Lately I have had the opportunity of seeing something of the good work being done among seamen, so many thousands of whom visit our port. In the Church of the Sea and Land, Market, corner of Henry street, Rev. Edward Hopper, D. D., pastor, I found a very large number at the weekly prayer-meeting, and learned that the work of grace among the seamen was going on without intermission. In the old Mariner's Church, corner of Madison and Catharine streets, Rev. E. D. Murphy, pastor, there has been a powerful work going on for two years, and thousands of sailors have been reached through missionary efforts.

The Children's Aid Society, in its lodging-houses for homeless boys, is doing an admirable work. The First Ward Reading-Room for Workingmen, located in the upper part of the De Witt Chapel, 135 Greenwich street, is a bright, cheery place, and attracts to its pleasant rooms hundreds of the class for whom it was designed. Jerry McAuley is constantly picking up the poor fellows drifting through the low places of Water street, and the Carmel Chapel, 134 Bowery, extends a helping hand to the wandering men who have lost their way.

If any one would like to see and hear of the progress that Gospel Temperance is making among these men, let them visit Carmel Chapel, 134 Bowery, on Monday evening, or Calvary Chapel, 153 Worth street, on Tuesday evening, or De Witt Chapel, 135 Greenwich street, on Wednesday evening. Let our good people visit the charitable institutions, and examine in detail the work as it is in progress, that they may form an intelligent judgment of their merits, and so be better prepared to distribute their patronage.

## XXV.

### WORKINGMEN'S CLUBS.

THE promoters of the workingmen's club movement appeal to the public for contributions in aid of the Lebanon Club. The movement is not designed to add to the *charities* of New York, but to furnish workingmen with healthy, moral, Christian forms of entertainment and instruction, and places of resort where they may be free from the vicious and degrading influences to which they are exposed

## WORKINGMEN'S CLUBS.

by their present only available resorts—the rum-shops. The men themselves will sustain the clubs when once they have been established by their friends. The success of the clubs in England, especially in London and Liverpool, and the fact that the work here is advised and supported by some of the most prominent men among our clergy and laity, who have been connected with and have witnessed the results of the work there, is a guarantee of the like success here.

"The Christian world is doing wrong in not doing more, not only in charity, but in sympathy," was the impressive remark of Rev. Dr. John Cotton Smith, at a meeting in his church for the encouragement of the plan which has proved so successful in England and in this country, the establishment of workingmen's clubs, not distinctly religious, and by no means with the aspect of charity institutions, but with pleasant apartments and appliances, conversation-rooms, refreshment-rooms, and smoking-rooms where all would be welcome and at home, without the dangerous allurements of the saloon and grogshops. It is feasible and practical, and, as was stated by Dr Rylance, who was familiar with the work in London, has rescued many from the ginshops. Christian employers and philanthropists could in no way better counteract the seditious measures of agitators and demagogues, who are embittering the minds of the workingmen, than by multiplying among them these healthful and attractive resorts, as expressions of real sympathy between these two classes rather than the antagonism which is claimed to exist.

## XXVI.

### *TENEMENT-HOUSES.*

A TENEMENT-HOUSE, as defined by the law of the state, includes "every house, building, or portion thereof, which is rented, leased, let, or hired out to be occupied, or is occupied as the house or residence of more than three families living independently of each other, and doing their cooking upon the premises, or by more than two families upon a floor, so living and cooking, but having a common right to the halls, stairways, yards, water-closets, or privies or some of them."

This is a description of a tenement-house of minimum size, and gives no adequate conception of the great mass of the tenement-houses of New York. In general they are old structures which were built for other purposes, partitioned off within so as to give each family two rooms, a living-room ten by twelve feet, and a bedroom six by four feet, while no regard is paid to ventilation or domestic conveniences. Twenty, thirty, forty, to one hundred and fifty such apartments are constructed, and in each a family of from three to five persons is crowded. Dangerous as is such overcrowding in individual houses when exposed to the full play of the wind, the danger is increased one hundred-fold when such dwellings are as closely packed together in the blocks as are the people in their apartments. Rear tenement-houses aggravate the evil beyond measure. They are built upon the rear of the yard, close to the rear tenement of the opposite lot, leaving a small, cold, and damp space between the front and rear houses, not inappropriately called the "well-hole." Not only are fresh air and sunlight thus effectually excluded from the living and sleeping apartments of most of the inmates, but the buildings become cold and damp, and in time are saturated with the poisonous and filthy excreta of the inmates. While the wood and other materials of such structures undergo the process of dry-rot, the wretched tenants waste and die from a disease expressively termed "tenement-house rot."

The debasing effects of such houses has never

been overdrawn. Perhaps the most vivid picture of the moral and physical degradation of this class of people was sketched by N. P. Willis immediately after the riots of 1863, who was an eyewitness to what he so truthfully describes. He says:

"The high, brick blocks and closely-packed houses in this neighborhood seemed to be literally hives of sickness and vice. Curiosity to look on at the fire raging so near them brought every inhabitant to the porch or window, or assembled them in ragged and dirty groups on the sidewalks in front. Probably not a creature who could move was left in-doors at that hour. And it is wonderful to see and difficult to believe that so much misery and disease and wretchedness can be huddled together and hidden by high walls, unvisited and unthought of, so near our own abodes. The lewd, but pale and sickly young women, scarce decent in their ragged attire, were impudent, and scattered everywhere in the crowd. But what numbers of these poorer classes are deformed, what numbers are made hideous by self-neglect and infirmity, and what numbers are paralytics, drunkards, imbecile, or idiotic, forlorn in their poverty-stricken abandonmemt for this world! Alas, human faces look so hideous with hope and vanity all gone! And female form and features are made so frightful by sin, squalor, and debasement! To walk the streets as we walked them, for those hours of conflagration and riot, was like a fearful witnessing of the day of judgment, with every wicked thing revealed, every hidden horror and abomination laid bare before hell's expectant fire."

The degree of overcrowding in our present tenement-house districts exceeds that of any of the large cities of the civilized world. The following comparative table exhibits the population to the square acre of the tenement-house classes, or the poor of New York and London, according to the census of 1870:

| NEW YORK. | | LONDON. | |
|---|---|---|---|
| Ward 11 | 328 | Strand | 307 |
| Ward 13 | 311 | St. Luke's | 259 |
| Ward 14 | 275 | East London | 266 |
| Ward 17 | 289 | Holborn | 229 |

The effect of this excessive crowding in badly-constructed dwellings upon the death-rate, is exhibited in the fact that this half of the population of New York yields seventy-five per cent. of the total annual sickness and mortality. Sickness and death are, however, but a fraction of the sum total of damage which overcrowding and defective house accommodations do to the poor. They are compelled to live in such familiar contact, such daily and nightly exposure of sexes, almost bestial, and such utter disregard of the common decencies of rational beings, that vice and the grossest immorality pervade the very atmosphere of their homes.

Examples illustrating the importance of reconstructing tenement-houses are numerous. A house in East Seventeenth street, having a capacity for ten families, had fallen into a condition of extreme dilapidation and filth. It was long occupied by the poorest and most depraved classes, when, in addition to other diseases, typhus fever began to prevail among the inmates, and in the course of six months twenty persons had this disease. It was then vacated and thoroughly repaired; the privies and drains were placed in good order; the walls were scraped and replastered; the woodwork was renewed; through and through ventilation in every room was secured; and the whole was neatly painted. During the five succeeding years scarcely a case of sickness occurred in that house.

The Old Brewery was formerly occupied by the lowest class of people living about the Five Points. It was in an extreme degree of dilapidation, and saturated with filth of every description. Every form of contagious disease here found a natural home and diseases directly traceable to local causes prevailed throughout the year. The death-rate of this community was about fifty-five per thousand, and the sickness-rate was nearly equal to the total population. This building was taken possession of by the Methodist Society, and converted into a mission-house. The interior was entirely remodelled, additions were made, and two stories of the old building were converted into living-rooms for families, each family having one living-room and one or two bedrooms, according to their necessities, with adequate ventilation. The capacity of these two stories was for twenty families. The families which occupy this portion of the reconstructed Old Brewery are of the same grade as those which formerly occupied this building. They are the most destitute and abandoned class of that district. The Mission gives them apartments free of rent, provided they conform strictly to the rules of the institution, and support themselves. These rules require that no liquors shall be drank by the inmates, nor brought into the house; perfect cleanliness of their persons, apartments, and halls, shall be preserved; they shall retire and rise at a given hour, etc. The results are surprising. There is not more than one death annually among these twenty families, and that from chronic diseases not traceable to the house, and but rarely is there a case of sickness.

The most immediately practicable measures of relief to overcrowding and its evils are of four kinds, namely: 1. Improvement and reconstruction of existing tenement-houses. 2. The building of model tenement-houses. 3. Providing cheap railroad transit. 4. The conversion of warehouses and other unused buildings into tenement-houses.

### IMPROVEMENT IN EXISTING TENEMENT-HOUSES.

The facts which have been given concerning the tenement-houses of this city will, it is hoped, awaken the attention of thoughtful men and raise inquiry as to means and measures of reform.

Plans have been projected at various times looking to improved dwellings for the poor, and some experiments have been made—as that of the "Workingmen's Home" in Elizabeth street, near Canal street, and at other places, and building associations have done something in establishing homes for mechanics in the suburbs of the city. While large-hearted philanthropists are combining with capitalists to devise and carry out grand schemes of improved dwellings for the poor, it may

## TENEMENT-HOUSES.

more readily meet the means and wishes of those who cannot enlist in any great undertaking to be informed of a wise and practicable plan that requires very little money. As for instance a good missionary woman, laboring among the poor at the Five Points and feeling deeply the evil influences surrounding those who are trying to lead a virtuous life, took a tenement-house, on her own responsibility, and put it in good order, and then introduced into it tenants of her own selection, who would be willing to conform to the ordinary rules of cleanliness and good behavior. It has been found that order and comfort and thrift are the result, and a visit to the house will be sufficient to convince any one of the practicability of this undertaking. In view of what has thus been demonstrated, it would seem to be entirely feasible to institute some very practical reforms in the tenement-houses as they are, and I respectfully submit if this is not worthy the attention of your readers. At the same time I would most respectfully and earnestly urge upon capitalists and others the necessity of larger and more comprehensive measures of permanent relief. If any will inquire further of the good work in progress at the Five Points, let them correspond with the City Missionary, 155 Worth street.

## XXVII.

### *OUR DANGER*

At the Forty-seventh Anniversary of the Society, the Rev. Dr. John Hall, spoke of the dangers to which society is exposed.

Dr. Hall said that he was to speak of the danger to the community, from that point of view which Christian citizens might be supposed to take. He contemplated moral and spiritual danger; but that peril is so intimately connected with others as to call for attention, and some solicitude, from every citizen, whether influenced by Christian or only by patriotic feeling, whether actuated by public spirit or only by intelligent regard to personal interests. There is danger from the growth of a large godless population outside the churches, uninfluenced by them, without the restraints and motives of religion. It is warrantable to say, "outside the churches," for by common consent the overwhelming proportion of crime is outside the churches—outside the Protestant churches. It is not claimed that all inside the churches are genuine and immaculate, nor all outside bad; but it is claimed that the outside classes furnish the criminals, as a whole. There are prisons in the land, he would venture to say, that had been long and fully occupied, that rarely had a professing Christian in them, in the technical Protestant sense of that word. Let this outside class grow up, and what must the effect be? The general tone of moral feeling must be lowered. The amount of temptation to the untainted must continually increase. There are many kinds of vice that eat themselves out, and must be constantly recruited from the innocent. The human birds and beasts of prey do not thrive on one another, but on the outside community. These corrupt classes constitute the ready tools of all schemers, demagogues, and enemies of the country. The suffrage gives them power; lack of principle makes them venal and unscrupulous in the use of means; and they can render, if only numerous enough and organized, the finest theoretic institutions nugatory for all the ends of freedom, security, and prosperity. Among them, institutions of vice and all mischievous agencies thrive; and the rich men who said of them, "Am I my brother's keeper?" will awaken to their existence and their awful force, when they find their sons and their daughters drawn into the vortex of their iniquity, and ruined.

There is danger to the Church—danger of her demoralization—by her coming to accept this state of things as an inevitable necessity of large cities. There is danger of our gliding into the infidel position, that there is heathenism which the truth cannot reach; that there is darkness so dense that the light cannot penetrate it; that there are problems too hard for Christian wisdom; that the Gospel which conquered old-world heathenism, is unequal to the conflict with its modern representatives.

The human mind easily becomes accustomed to evil; ceases to be shocked by it; is no longer horrified; learns to say, "Of course, there is a fearful amount of vice and sin;" and to say it in an airy, jaunty way, as we might comment upon fogs off Newfoundland, or stormy weather about January. So our hearts get deadened to all the dreadful results involved, in time and in eternity, and we seem to act as if the men and women who are not fit to live with us, not fit for freedom, not fit for any place but prisons and penitentiaries, will be somehow quite fit for that holy and eternal home into which nothing entereth that defileth, or worketh abominations, or maketh a lie!

Now, whose business is this? It is the business of all American citizens. These great cities influence the destinies of a country because mind sharpens mind, concert and organization are here easy, and men can move in imposing masses. The ballot-box can be used or abused, and physical force can be easily employed to intimidate the feeble and overbear the hesitating.

All property owners in this city have an interest in this. I am aware, said the speaker, that even for evil purposes houses can bring in for a while a high income; but it is only for a while. There is a retributive law at work here, and the owners who are conveniently blind to the uses to which their property is put and by which they reap the profits, become losers eventually through the bad odor into which neighborhoods fall. I know the man who was invited as pastor to a church in this city, who made examination, and found so many disreputable houses around as to seriously interfere with its prosperity and his decision—and that was not below Fourteenth street.

All employers have an interest in this question, as they will find out when dealing with the unprincipled and the violent, instead of the intelligent and the God-fearing working-people. Let there grow up a large class of the kind described, and they will work only when it cannot be helped: they will prescribe their own terms; they will not shrink from violence in enforcing them; they will become the ready instruments of the designing; they will be too thoughtless to judge of the statements made to them; and too ignorant of the principles that underlie social life to hold back from any demand however preposterous.

## XXVIII.

### *TRIED AND PROVED.*

In various ways the problem of city evangelization is proposed to be solved, as witness the discussions in Christian conventions and the essays in the current literature of the day.

One will have it that the true way to reach the people with the gospel is to make all the seats in all the churches absolutely free to all comers. Another is equally certain that the people will never come to the churches as they are, free or not free. Theatres must be opened or gospel halls be built, relieved from all church conventionalities and restrictions.

We admire the enthusiasm with which these

and many other plans are advocated, and look with interest upon the various experiments which are being made in bringing the gospel to bear upon the hearts of multitudes of the non-churchgoing people in our great cities.

If any inquire what has actually been done in this direction, it may be answered that for fifty years and more men and women of the various Protestant churches have been quietly and unostentatiously and patiently going into the poorer quarters, through the streets and lanes of the city, telling the story of the Saviour's love, cheering the sad, instructing the ignorant, and directing the wandering to the sinner's friend. As they have won the confidence of those they sought to benefit, they have led the young into Sabbath-schools and Bible classes and the adults into churches, wherever free accommodations were available.

In some parts of the city where no Protestant churches are found, and in other districts where none are easy of access, chapels have been built, neat, commodious, and church-like, where the Christian minister and the Christian ordinances are found, and where the poorest may come without fear of intruding. These chapels are not stigmatized as missions—they are not placarded as such—they are not known as such among the people who care for them. The people speak of these humble places of worship as churches or chapels with as much interest and affection as any of their well-to-do brethren speak of their own fine churches on the avenue. The families in the chapels we are speaking of are taught to contribute of their means to the support of the gospel, and do, in fact, give a fair proportion according to their ability, and thus, equally with the rich, enjoy the privilege of paying for what they get. Thus in every way the self-respect of the people is preserved, and they learn to help themselves.

And not only so, but they naturally and quickly learn to help others, and take up the work of evangelization themselves. A man, brought into one of these chapels, and finding a pleasant Sabbath home, and Christian kindness and sympathy, and congenial society, instantly becomes a zealous propagandist, and sets to work to bring his neighbors with him, and these in turn again will bring others. Just as at the first opening of the Christian church, when Andrew went after Peter and Philip went after Nathanael.

The point we are making is this: while plans and methods of city evangelization are being discussed, and experiments of one sort and another are being tried, here is one way that is economical, wise, tried, and sure, namely, the plan of city missions, according to which Christian men and women, in the spirit of Christ and for the love of Christ, are going to the homes of the people, and winning a place in the hearts of the people for the gospel they carry by the gospel lives they are living; and so are drawing them into churches and building them up into efficient agents for carrying on the good work.

It may be objected that this plan requires time and money, and that it is too slow in its operation. And we need only reply that a thorough, permanent work like this is worth all it costs, and is not too slow to be sure.

Whether the work of city evangelization is as expensive as is alleged, may be judged of by such figures as these: the New York City Mission has, during the fifty years of its beneficent activities, spent $20,000 a year in sustaining its missionary operations, and for the same period has been instrumental in the hopeful conversion of five hundred souls a year.

Of course the majority of these converts have passed away, but of the living we have knowledge of many that adorn the doctrine of God their Saviour, some of whom are occupying positions of eminent usefulness in the gospel ministry and elsewhere. Though the formation of churches is comparatively a recent development of city evangelization, churches of 400, 500, 600, and 800 members are found, with a vigorous spiritual life, exerting a power for good upon all around them.

In two instances, as the result of the continuous, persistent, well-directed efforts of intelligent Christian workers for fifteen years, the work has outgrown its first accommodation, and new, commodious, and even elegant buildings, have been erected, the better to meet the increased demands of the enterprise. And as an indication of the growth of confidence in this sort of work, it may be said that the first mission building erected cost perhaps $25,000 or $30,000, while the new ones cost $80,000 to $100,000 each. There are chapels now, of ten years' standing, that are found altogether inadequate to accommodate the people that are ready to be gathered in.

In the light of such facts as these, is it not fair to assume that this proposition has been demonstrated, namely, that, given a neat, commodious chapel, with an intelligent, attractive preacher, and warm-hearted, efficient helpers, churches and Sabbath-schools can be gathered, and powerful agencies for good can be set in operation in any destitute neighborhood? To any one who has the means there is offered this grand opportunity, namely, to give one thousand dollars a year, which, on the average, will support a city missionary, who, on no less a testimony than that of Lord Shaftesbury, is equal, as a moral police force, to one hundred policemen; and after he is done using his money, he may leave fifty thousand dollars, which will plant a chapel that will be a well of salvation to untold multitudes for all time to come.

## XXIX.

### *TESTIMONIES.*

At the recent Anniversary several of the pastors of the City Mission chapels presented the more prominent features of their work, giving altogether an impressive exhibition of the practical operations of city evangelization. The Rev. George Hatt, of De Witt Chapel, who has seen forty years of city missionary service, spoke on the importance and utility of tracts in Christian labor, and related many interesting facts in illustration. A man who received a tract on the Battery Park came to the chapel and found Christ there; then brought his wife, who also found Christ; and for years that man has been laboring for souls. A tract entitled, "The Act of Faith," given to a sick man, led to his conversion. The missionary sent a tract entitled, "What art Thou?" to a young man in whom he felt deeply interested. It was the means of the young man's conviction, and so of his conversion; and that convert is now an elder in a New Jersey church. On another occasion the speaker sent a tract to a young man anonymously. The recipient was going to the opera on the night he received the silent messenger; but it was God's arrow of conviction, and went to his heart. He came to Christ, and then taking the tract to Sunday-school, read it, and related the circumstances connected with his reception of it. Two of the teachers were moved to seek the Saviour through the simple recital.

Rev. James Marshall, of Lebanon Chapel, said he had a parish of 140,000 souls, and believed, among other plans, it was necessary to find some means of getting people under range of the gospel artillery. Lebanon Chapel, like a magnet gathering the steel-filings out of surrounding dust, had gathered many precious souls out of the mass of sin and impurity, but there were thousands as yet unreached.

Rev. John Dooly, of the Carmel Chapel, Bowery, said the Tenth and Fourteenth wards, in which he labored, contained 68,000 persons, including 12,000 children. They had nine Protestant churches, twelve Sabbath-schools, and 1,000 drink-shops. Through the past six years nine hundred persons had professed conversion in connection with the work. The speaker could tell of many trophies. In one case a man was brought to the prayer-meeting by a former comrade in crime—they were both burglars. The older one came out of curiosity, but was laid under conviction of sin and knelt in prayer for pardon. The praying groups contained the missionary and saved thief on one side and a seeking thief on the other, and the latter found the Saviour. He had a "jimmy" and skeleton-keys in his sleeve, intending to break into a house that night. These he gave to the missionary, and they were now in the Society's office.

Rev. A. F. Schauffler, of Olivet Chapel, dwelt on the necessity of extended effort in Sunday-school work down town, as only by taking hold of the children could the masses be reached. Children needed no forcing; they would come to school gladly. Indeed, hundreds of them had been turned away for want of room. New York Christians must send their best workers into these mission Sabbath-schools, as the work required the best possible ability. A dying mother told her boy that the Lord Jesus would come to him and take care of him when she died. All night he waited at her grave, and in the morning a gentleman seeing him, asked and heard his story, then told him the Lord Jesus had sent him. "You have been a long while coming," the little fellow replied; and the poor, destitute, down-town children might well say to Christian people, "You have been a long time coming to us and bringing Jesus with you to our hearts and homes."

The Rev. Charles S. Robinson, D. D., asserted that we did not understand the masses; they were human like ourselves, and we could do them good if we would give them our hearts and our time. A plank was shoved to a drowning man, but as he touched it his fingers slipped and down he went. This was repeated more than once, when with an almost dying effort he called out to his would-be deliverers to give him the wood-end of the plank.

They found out that the plank was covered with ice at one end, and so the poor fellow's hands had slipped off every time he tried to grasp it. Getting hold of the other end, he was rescued. Let us give something better than the ice-end of the plank to distressed humanity, something more than the cold sympathy of formal charity. They want warm hearts and a sympathy that they feel to be genuine, and they will respond.

The following resolutions were submitted by Mr. Roswell C. Smith, and seconded by Mr. Thomas F. Jeremiah, and unanimously and heartily adopted by the meeting:

"1. That history and experience have fully confirmed the wisdom and efficiency of the principles and the plans of city evangelization.

"2. That in the New York City Mission and Tract Society we recognize an agency, well-established and intelligently directed, and admirably adapted to the work of carrying the gospel to the homes and the hearts of the people.

"3. That the moral and social condition of the multitudes in this city calls for the most vigorous and persistent prosecution of all Christian means and measures for their elevation and improvement.

"4. That we heartily welcome the earnest co-operation of the ladies in city mission work, believing that the labors of the missionary women under their direction among the wives and mothers and children of the poor are of inestimable importance in the renovation of society."

### AUXILIARY MEASURES.

PRACTICAL and thoughtful philanthropists are continually turning over in their thoughts the questions that touch the moral and social condition of the working classes, and now and then a good idea takes a practical shape, which at once commends itself to the judgment of every good citizen. Among the projects now on foot is that styled the "Workingmen's Club." It should be understood that this is a movement not designed to add to the charities of New York, but to furnish workingmen with healthy, moral, Christian forms of entertainment and instruction, and places of resort where they may be free from the vicious and degrading influences of the drinking saloons. It is supposed that the workingmen themselves will be ready to sustain these clubs when they have been established by their friends. The Rev. Dr. Rylance, who has personal knowledge of similar clubs in London, Rev. Dr. John Cotton Smith, Rev. Dr. Henry C. Potter, and others, have given their endorsement of the plan, and members of the Executive Committee of the City Mission are looking after the development of the same, and we trust it will not be long before a good beginning will be made.

Another very practical, common-sense undertaking is that of taking a tenement-house, and after a thorough cleaning, putting into it tenants who will be willing to conform to the ordinary rules of cleanliness, sobriety, and good behavior. A laborious missionary, visiting daily among the poor at the Five Points, feeling deeply the evil influences surrounding those who are trying to lead a virtuous life, took a tenement-house on her own responsibility, and with broom and brush, and whitewash and paint, thoroughly renovated the place, and then introduced tenants who would promise to keep their rooms in order, close the doors at reasonable hours, and shut out intoxicating drinks; and the experiment proves that order and comfort and thrift are the result, to the great advantage of both landlord and tenant. It would seem that this comparatively inexpensive reform might be set on foot all over the city, among all the tenement-houses, if only some good, energetic man or woman would take hold of the idea and urge it forward.

One of the most difficult problems is, What shall be done for the strong, willing men who are out of work, and who, to keep from starvation, must be aided by charity? A suggestion has been made that a farm be purchased convenient to the city, to which may be sent young men of good character, who are temporarily destitute, requiring them while there to labor eight hours per day, provide each with working clothes while on the farm, clean and mend their own clothing during their stay, and return the same to them when they leave. Organize a class for special training in the details of agriculture, and thereby increase the number of practical farmers. A plan like this, carried out with skill and tact, would give a man a chance to earn his meat and drink, and to gain such physical strength that if a call came for a strong man he would be able to respond. He remains on the farm until he hears from his friends, from an employer who is ready to give him work, or until some other place is found for him.

The Gospel Temperance movement, another project of present interest, is spreading among workingmen with a good deal of encouragement.

Meetings are held at various points around the city, and hundreds of men are signing the temperance pledge. If any would look into Carmel Chapel, 134 Bowery, on Monday evening, Calvary Chapel, 153 Worth street, on Tuesday evening, De Witt Chapel, 135 Greenwich street, on Wednesday evening, they would be able to see for themselves the character of these services and the interest felt in them.

Christian men, employers, and others, could not do a wiser thing than to give their hearty and generous support to these and other like enterprises, by which a real and practical sympathy for the working classes may be shown in the most effective way. Correspondence is invited from those who have the means and the disposition to aid either or any of these projects, and further information of plans and methods will be freely given to those who may be interested.

## XXX.

## *WOMAN'S WORK IN CITY MISSIONS.*

### ORGANIZATION OF THE FEMALE BRANCH.

#### OFFICERS AND MANAGERS.

##### OFFICERS.

Mrs. Z. S. Ely, First Directress, 26 West Twenty-sixth street.
Mrs. Horace Holden, Second Directress, 15 West Twelfth street.
Mrs. John L. Mason, Treasurer, Brooklyn.
Miss F. L. Baker, Assistant Treasurer, 163 West Eleventh street.
Mrs. F. A. Conkling, Secretary, 27 East Tenth street.
Mrs. A. R. Brown, Superintendent, 50 Bible House.

##### MANAGERS.

###### SOUTH REFORMED CHURCH.

Mrs. J. A. Bennett, 3 East Thirty-third street.
Miss Louisa Weed, 55 East Twenty-first street.

### MADISON SQUARE CHURCH.

Mrs. William A. Hallock, 132 West Thirteenth street.
Mrs. Z. S. Ely, 26 West Twenty-sixth street.
Mrs. J. C. Ely, 6 East Thirtieth street.

### FIFTH AVENUE PRESBYTERIAN CHURCH.

Mrs. Loring Andrews, 139 Fifth avenue.
Mrs. B. Brown, 117 East Fourteenth street.
Mrs. M. K. Jesup, 197 Madison avenue.
Miss S. J. Lee, 161 West Thirty-fourth street.
Mrs. Wm. Libbey, 47 Park avenue.
Mrs. C. P. Britton, 12 East Fifty-fourth street.
Mrs. E. S. Jaffray, 615 Fifth avenue.

### BRICK CHURCH.

Mrs. Horace Holden, 15 West Twelfth street.
Miss Sophia Ely, 117 East Thirty-seventh street.
Miss Whitlock, 460 West Twenty-third street.

### THIRTY-FOURTH STREET REFORMED CHURCH.

Mrs. Henry Camerden, Jr., 358 West Thirty-first street.

### COLLEGIATE REFORMED CHURCH, FIFTH AVENUE, COR. TWENTY-NINTH STREET.

Mrs. J. P. White, 224 Madison avenue.

### MEMORIAL CHURCH, MADISON AVENUE AND FIFTY-THIRD STREET.

Mrs. R. M. Field, 139 East Forty-fifth street.
Miss G. B. Henry, 73 East Fifty-fourth street.

### UNIVERSITY PLACE PRESBYTERIAN CHURCH.

Mrs. Charles A. Davison, 8 West Forty-eighth street.
Mrs. F. A. Burrall, 28 West Eleventh street.
Miss Helen Turnbull, 5 West Sixteenth street.

### FIRST PRESBYTERIAN CHURCH, FIFTH AVENUE, COR. ELEVENTH STREET.

Mrs. James McLanahan, 33 West Twentieth street.

### BROADWAY TABERNACLE.

Mrs. Joseph E. Case, 19 West Fiftieth street.
Mrs. Clark Bell, 30 West Fifty-first street.
Miss L. G. Satterlee, 221 West Forty-second st.
Miss M. S. Bugbee, 45 West Thirty-fifth street.

### COLLEGIATE REFORMED CHURCH, FIFTH AVENUE, COR. OF FORTY-EIGHTH STREET.

Mrs. S. H. Mead, 674 Madison avenue.

### FOURTH PRESBYTERIAN CHURCH, WEST THIRTY-FOURTH STREET.

Mrs. James Stuart, 27 East Thirty-seventh st.
Mrs. F. Blume, 146 West Fifteenth street.

### CHURCH OF THE COVENANT.

Mrs. Wm. E. Dodge, 225 Madison avenue.
Miss Emma Sutherland, 336 Lexington avenue.
Miss Mary Crosby, 150 Lexington avenue.

### CHURCH OF ENGLEWOOD, NEW JERSEY.

Miss Olivia Hoadley, Englewood, N. J.
Miss Mary N. Wright, 45 West Thirty-fifth st.

### LUTHERAN CHURCH OF THE HOLY TRINITY, WEST TWENTY-FIRST STREET.

Mrs. Louis S. J. Brewster, 28 West Fifty-seventh street.

### EXECUTIVE COMMITTEE.

Mrs. B. Brown, 117 East Fourteenth street.
Mrs. M. K. Jesup, 197 Madison avenue.
Mrs. H. Holden, 15 West Twelfth street.
Mrs. Wm. A. Hallock, 132 West Thirteenth st.
Miss S. Lee, 161 West Thirty-fourth street.

### MISSIONARIES.

1. Mrs. Lefler, 65 Orchard street.
2. Mrs. Ward, 70 Columbia street.

3. Mrs. Rogers, 194 Prince street.
4. Miss Vantine 409 West Nineteenth street.
5. Mrs. Van Morsten, 107 First avenue.
6. Mrs. Wisner, 63 Second street.
7. Miss McDonald, 50 Bible House.
8. Miss Eighmey, 55 East Ninth street.
9. Mrs. Miller, 55 East Ninth street.
10. Miss Monroe, 55 East Ninth street.
11. Miss Smyth, 55 East Ninth street.
12. Miss Dye, 55 East Ninth street.
13. Miss March, 55 East Ninth street.
14. Miss Root, 50 Bible House.
15. Mrs. Miles, 155 Worth street.
16. Miss Dow, 55 East Ninth street.
17. Miss Gumbart, 55 East Ninth street.
18. Miss Miller, 55 East Ninth street.
19. Miss Post, 55 East Ninth street.
20. Mrs. Barnum, 55 East Ninth street.
21. Mrs. Sloat, 55 East Ninth street.

## STATEMENT OF THE WORK OF MISSIONARY WOMEN.

FIFTY-FIVE years ago this Society began its work of sending the Gospel's invitation to the ignorant and depraved of New York city.

The names of all those who, on that March morning in 1822, met in Mrs. Bethune's parlor to plan its organization, are now graven in marble. "They rest from their labors," and we have entered into them.

The increased area of the city since that time, and the change in the character of its inhabitants, made necessary the employment of paid instead of volunteer workers, but has not diminished the power or the importance of a Christian woman's influence; and the results of these many years show plainly that no agency exists better calculated to reach and elevate those whose lines have fallen outside the influence of church and pastor.

### AIMS AND METHODS.

It would seem quite unnecessary, after so many years, to define the aims of this Society; yet hardly a week passes in which the question does not come in some form, "What do your visitors do?"

Many seem to regard our work synonymous with that of the Society for Improving the Condition of the Poor. We do not so consider it. Though there are cases where the body's claims must be *first* attended to, these are not nearly as frequently met as we once supposed; and experience confirms more and more strongly our faith in the truth, "Seek first the kingdom of God and his righteousness, and these things shall be added."

Some time since a poor woman in a neighboring village hearing that a lady to whom she had looked for assistance was about to remove, despairingly exclaimed, "What shall we do? We will have no one now to depend on but the Lord." We have met many who have seen one prop after another removed, till feeling that none was left but God, have learned there was none like him.

Sin being the cause of all our woes, our chief aim is to lead the people to see and realize this, and then to urge the remedy. This is no routine work. When well done it calls into exercise all of the powers and ingenuity of the most capable.

During the last year we have labored much to improve the quality of our work, by the study of God's Word; by greater efforts for thoroughness; by meetings for conference and comparing experiences in the work; and prayer for God's blessing. While this manner of working may not tend to the increase of numbers in statistics, we believe the record above is more sure to be "well done."

## HOUSE TO HOUSE VISITATION.

To the influence of our devoted band of workers in the homes of the poor, we look for our greatest success. There we touch the inner life, and can suit the message to individual souls. One who has only heard described life in a tenement-house, knows little of the great obstacles in the way of Christian living among the very poor. The impure air of a crowded room is quite as detrimental to spiritual as to animal life. How can children, who spend their lives either on the sidewalk or crowded into one little room, to which their father comes home nightly too much intoxicated to know what he says or does, grow up with any sense of propriety, or any purity.

We are looking forward, with earnest hope of some relief, to the time when rapid transit will become an accomplished fact; and watch with great interest the growth of public opinion, in appreciation of the necessity that something should be done to improve the homes of the lower classes. We believe that many are convinced, and the question now is not, "Is there need that anything be done?" but "What?" and "How?" We do not ask for "model" homes, only that some already built be improved in ventilation, and placed in competent hands to order and control. Nothing would assist more in the moral elevation of the people than some practical move in this direction.

The lack of employment during the last year has led many into temptations which have been barriers in our way. Many have "regarded every day alike" when they could get work, justifying their disregard of holy time, saying, "Our first duty is to get bread for our children." Notwithstanding these and other drawbacks, our work has steadily progressed.

Men who, for seven, fifteen, and twenty years, have neglected the house of God, have been brought there, and we have been permitted to see the transforming power of religion in many families where formerly there was no thought beyond the want or pleasure of the present hour.

These changes are not wrought by a solitary call or admonition, but each has cost many a weary journey to the "top floor," many a word of warning and earnest prayer, many a season of discouragement; but when, by the blessing of God, the reward has come, the labor is accounted as nothing.

### OUR WORKERS.

Twenty-five different missionaries have been in the employ of our Society during the year.

After two or three months' trial, some have retired on account of insufficient strength. One, who had been with us some time, was called to a specific work in which she felt peculiar interest. One who received a severe injury from a baseball thrown in the street, is at present laid aside. Another has temporarily retired to acquire greater fitness. And we close the year with the same number we began it, seventeen.

### MISSIONARY NURSE.

A new power for good has been introduced this year, the Missionary Nurse. Prepared in the Training School, she is thoroughly competent to do all that is necessary in cases of extreme illness, and has been an unspeakable comfort to many who had no one to minister to them.

We hope before long others will join us in this capacity, for a wide field is open for usefulness in this way.

### MOTHERS' MEETINGS.

Our weekly prayer-meetings for mothers, held in the afternoon, have numbered in attendance from fifteen to twenty in the smallest, to two hundred.

The hour spent at these meetings is often the only one during the week when a weary woman can break off from her daily duties to listen to God's message of love to her. The baby in her arms is no hindrance to her enjoyment. The quiet alone would be very welcome to her, but what power of healing for her spirit in the "Word" distinctly read and carefully explained. On Thanksgiving day, one of our German workers invited the women of her meeting to bring their husbands with them, as many would have a holiday. They came through the pouring rain, many without umbrellas, till over two hundred and seventy were gathered to give thanks to God—for what?

Some were very thinly clad, and many of them had often during the year suffered hunger. What had they to be thankful for?

As the leader showed those fathers and mothers what cause for gratitude they had, in their own lives spared to their children, and the children to them; that the word of God in its blessed promises had so quickened and established their faith; and more than all, for the riches many of them had found in Christ Jesus; their hearty appreciation of her words was written on their faces, softening the deep care-lines.

As she closed, all who could cordially respond to the sentiments expressed were asked to stand. They rose as one, and joined in singing, "Oh, for a thousand tongues to sing."

Our English Mothers' Meetings are smaller, but not less prized.

### THE OPEN DOOR,

Formerly located in Sullivan street, now at 194 Prince street, still invites the straying ones to enter and learn of Him who said, "Go and sin no more."

During the summer Mrs. R—— who has it in charge, paid the penalty of overwork in a severe illness. She has hardly recovered her usual strength, but has resumed the women's meetings at the Tombs and in her house with very satisfactory results.

During the month of November ninety-five were brought into the house services, and the record of the meetings in the Tombs, the last seven weeks, gives an aggregate attendance of three hundred.

Weekly visits have been continued at the House

of Detention, though the number of women found there has been smaller than last year, sometimes not more than two or three.

### HELPING HANDS.

To the question how to carry on the temporal and spiritual work together, the Helping Hand gives a very satisfactory solution.

The "relief" received there is *earned* while the work of elevating and instructing goes on. These Associations are almost entirely under the care of ladies from different churches, who volunteer their services. The largest, in Olivet Chapel, has over forty ladies engaged in it, and gives assistance to three hundred poor women every winter. Our invaluable Englewood helpers are still unwavering in their devotion to the one in Lebanon Chapel, assuming its entire care and support.

Last summer these ladies extended to six of the poor women of their charge an invitation to spend a week in their beautiful village. When the week had passed, six others took their places. This was continued for six weeks, the ladies each in turn furnishing the necessary supplies.

The memory of that week of wonderful experience will be "a joy for ever" to those whose lives so seldom lead in pleasant paths.

The youngest of these sewing meetings, begun last winter in Calvary Chapel at the Five Points, showed so marked an influence on the women attending it, that it has been opened again this winter, though we know not from where the means are to come for its support. Nothing but lack of funds prevents our extending the benefits of this branch of our work to many more of those so urgent in their request for admission.

All of the money devoted to the Helping Hands is given for that purpose, and not taken from the regular contributions to the Society for the support of missionaries. The unflagging interest of the ladies engaged, some having continued eight years, shows their approbation of it; and the woman who said at the last week's meeting, "I am watching all of the week for Tuesday to come, it is the bright spot in my life," gave expression to the feelings of many.

### OUR HOME,

Which completed its first year in May, has fulfilled our hopes in the comfort it affords the Missionaries, and in the opportunity it gives for preparation of mind and heart for the important work we are doing. With nearly all other organizations we are feeling the hard times. During the last month the family has numbered sixteen, and when our ranks are again filled the Home will be filled also.

Early in the year the oldest member of the Society, Mrs. Thomas C. Doremus, fell asleep. The bent form so constantly in our meetings is seen by us no more. Her cheering words and rich experience are sadly missed, but we know that when the Lord comes with his saints we shall see her again.

To all who have so cordially assisted us we give hearty thanks. Hospitals have freely opened their doors to our sick, those who care for "Widows," "Orphans," "Half Orphans," the "Poor," the "Aged," the "Friendless," and the "Inebriate," have all kindly received those we have taken to them, and their coöperation is remembered gratefully.

Yet we have often met those for whom no place could be found, and we were obliged to let them slip back into their old haunts and habits. Satan is still "wiser than the children of light." His followers have located a saloon in a place convenient to the Blackwell's Island boat, where those who for longer or shorter time have been eating the bread of repentance in the Penitentiary, or recovering from the effects of an evil course in Charity Hospital, may prepare themselves for another term there. But Christian Charity lags behind, and does not lay a kind hand on the weak sister, piloting her by the slippery places. Why? Because among all our Homes there is no place where such may be taken. If real Christian love united with business capacity would but espouse the interests of this class, and open a Shelter for them, connecting with it a Laundry, we believe it might be made self-supporting, and prevent many a suicide. It should be a thoroughly Christian Home, to do the work for women which the one recently established seems to be accomplishing among men.

There is another class we feel might be easily reached were special effort made among them, and a place provided where they could earn a living. We refer to the colored girls, hundreds of whom are walking in the broadest part of the broad way that leads to death. Impulsive and vacillating by nature, they are easily led into good as well as evil, and removed from their surroundings till strength in well-doing had been acquired, many might be rescued.

We would express our earnest thanks to those

who have been our counsellors, as well as to our supporters and helpers; to the young friends in Sabbath-school classes out of town who have remembered our sick and suffering ones; to the Flower Mission which has so often filled our hands with bouquets for the Mothers' Meetings and sick-rooms; to Dr. Burrall who has by night or day rendered cheerfully such valuable service, to Drs. Parker and Stimson, and Duberceau, for assistance in special cases.

Above all, we render thanks to Him who has given us such abounding token of his approbation, in answered prayers, in sustaining grace, and the blessing of his presence. In his name our work is done, and to him be the praise and glory of its success, now and evermore.

## XXXI.

## *ORGANIZATION.*

### CONSTITUTION.

#### CHARTER.

*Passed February* 19, 1866, *and amended February* 24, 1870.

ACT. An Act of Incorporation.

TITLE. An Act to Incorporate THE NEW CITY MISSION AND TRACT SOCIETY.

The people of the state of New York, represented in Senate and Assembly, do enact as follows:

SECTION 1. George W. Abbe, Richard Amerman, Constant A. Andrews, Benjamin B. Atterbury, Josiah W. Baker, George W. Beale, Nathan Bishop, William T. Booth, Benjamin F. Butler, William A. Cauldwell, Charles C. Colgate, William W. Cornell, Hiram A. Crane, Stephen Cutter, Henry Day, William E. Dodge, Jr., Thomas C. Doremus, Zebulon S. Ely, Edward P. Griffin, Robert G. Hatfield, James C. Holden, Lewis Hallock, M. D., David Irwin, Thomas Jeremiah, Morris K. Jesup, Caleb B. Knevals, Leonard Hazeltine, Jr., Joseph B. Lockwood, Benjamin Lord, John R. Ludlow, A.

H. Turner, M. D., Almon Merwin, Walter T. Miller, Charles C. North, John E. Parsons, William Phelps, Alfred A. Post, Archibald Russell, Thomas S. Shepherd, Thomas Storm, William Johnston, Thomas M. Turlay, William Walker, A. R. Wetmore, Ralph Wells, Frederick W. Whittemore, Jacob F. Wyckoff, Milton St. John, John S. McLean, Horace Winans, and their associates, are hereby constituted a body corporate by the name of the New York City Mission and Tract Society, and by that name shall have the powers which by the third title of the eighteenth chapter of the first part of the Revised Statutes are declared to belong to corporations, and shall be capable of taking by purchase or devise, holding or conveying any estate, real or personal, for the use and purposes of said corporation, subject to any provisions of law in relation to devises and bequests by wills. Such real estate shall not exceed the yearly value of fifty thousand dollars.

SEC. 2. The objects of this corporation are to promote morality and religion among the poor and destitute of the city of New York, by the employment of missionaries, by the diffusion of evangelical reading and the sacred Scriptures, by the establishment of Sabbath-schools, mission stations and chapels, for the preaching of the gospel, and for other ordinances of Divine worship.

Sec. 3. The business affairs and estate of said corporation shall be managed by a Board of fifty Directors, who shall hold their office for one year, or until others are elected in their place. The first Board of Directors shall consist of the fifty persons named in the first section of this Act, and they shall hold their office until the Wednesday following the second Monday in December, one thousand eight hundred and sixty-six, and until their successors are chosen. After the year one thousand eight hundred and sixty-nine, the Board of Directors shall be composed and chosen from persons in communion with different religious denominations. All vacancies in the Board of Directors shall be filled as the By-Laws direct.

Sec. 4. There shall be an annual election for Directors on the Wednesday following the second Monday in December of each year, at which election each member of said corporation shall be entitled to cast one vote. There shall be such notice and inspection of election as the By-Laws direct. Any person who, within one year, has contributed ten dollars to the funds of the corporation, or who at any one time may have contributed twenty dollars, shall be entitled to vote at such annual election for Directors.

SEC. 5. At all meetings of the Board of Directors, seven members shall constitute a quorum for the transaction of business.

SEC. 6. The said corporation may make such By-Laws and rules for the regulation of its business, the management of its affairs, the choice, powers, and duties of its officers and agents, as are not inconsistent with its charter and the laws of the state.

This Act shall take effect immediately.

## BY-LAWS.

ARTICLE 1. The Board of Directors shall annually elect a President and a Vice-President. The President, or in his absence, the Vice-President, shall preside at the meetings of the Society and of the Board of Directors. If both of said officers be absent, a Chairman *pro tempore* shall be chosen. The Board may elect such persons as they think proper Honorary members of the Society.

ART. 2. The Board of Directors shall appoint a Corresponding Secretary, a Recording Secretary, a Treasurer, and a Superintendent of Missions, who shall hold office during the pleasure of the Board.

Art. 3. It shall be the duty of the Corresponding Secretary, under the direction of the Board, to conduct the correspondence of the Society and of the Board, to attend to the business of the office, the publication of statistics and documents, and the preparation of reports.

Art. 4. The Recording Secretary shall give notice of the meetings of the Board and of the Society, and shall record the Minutes of these meetings,

Art. 5. The Treasurer shall take charge of the funds, and report the state of the treasury at each regular meeting of the Board, and pay all bills of expenses incurred by the Society, when they shall have been examined and passed upon by the Executive Committee.

Art. 6. The Superintendent of Missions, under the direction of the Board, shall have a general oversight of the missionary work of the Society, carry out their instructions for the regulation of the missionaries, the establishment of mission stations, the appointment of preaching services; and shall present these objects to the churches.

Art. 7. The Board of Directors shall hold meetings quarterly in the months of January, April, July, and October of each year. They shall annually appoint the Executive Committee, and such other committees as may be called for from time to time.

Art. 8. The Executive Committee shall consist of eighteen members, including the Corresponding Secretary, the Treasurer, and the Superintendent of Missions, who shall be members *ex officio*, five of whom shall constitute a quorum.

It shall be their duty to locate the missions, to purchase, build, or hire such premises as are required for mission stations, and to make all necessary improvements and alterations in the same from time to time. They may lease such part of any mission station as is not needed by the Society, for purposes not inconsistent with the designs of the mission, and they may sell to any evangelical church or mission, or any other proper party, any station owned by the Society, when in their judgment it is for the best interest of the cause to do so. They shall appoint the missionaries required for the service of the Society, fix their salaries, direct their labors, and the services in the mission stations. They may appoint any agents whom they may find it expedient to employ in the business of the Society; they may form or acknowledge auxiliary societies, and establish the terms of connection between the auxiliaries and the Society; and in general are authorized to do whatever may be necessary to give efficiency to the work assigned them.

They shall have power to fill all vacancies in their own number. They shall annually choose out of their own number the following Standing Committees: a Finance Committee, a Building Committee, and a Missionary Committee, and they shall also choose a Visiting Committee for each month.

Any member of the Executive Committee absenting himself without leave from four consecutive meetings of the Committee, shall be considered as having resigned his seat, and the Committee shall proceed to fill the vacancy.

The Executive Committee shall make reports of their proceedings to the Board of Directors.

ART. 9. At meetings of the Board, the following shall be the order of business: 1. Prayer; 2. Minutes; 3. Unfinished Business; 4. Reports of Committees; 5. Reports of Missionaries; 6. Report of Superintendent of Missions; 7. Report of Treasurer; 8. Report of Secretary; 9. Elections; 10. New Business.

ART. 10. These By-Laws may be amended at any regular meeting of the Board of Directors, on the recommendation of the Executive Committee, by a vote of two-thirds of the members present.

## THE CHAPELS.

First Ward, De Witt Chapel, No. 135 Greenwich street, near Cedar street. Rev. George Hatt, pastor; Mr. James Farrow, assistant. The Mission Sabbath-school was organized in 1836, and the Mission service was commenced in 1852, and established in the present location in 1873. Sabbath services 10:30 A. M. and 7:30 P. M. Sabbath-school at 9 A. M. and 2 P. M. Prayer-meetings Tuesday and Thursday evenings. Temperance meeting, Wednesday evening.

There were reported last year 155 preaching services, with an attendance in the aggregate of 7,379; 308 prayer-meetings, with an attendance in the aggregate of 5,154; and in the Sunday-school 110 children received instruction during the year.

Sixth Ward, Calvary Chapel, No. 153 Worth street, adjoining House of Industry, near Centre street. Temporarily supplied by Mr. W. F. Barnard. This Chapel first opened for religious services, Sabbath evening, February 13, 1870. The church in Calvary Chapel was organized February, 1871. Sabbath services 10:30 A. M. and 7:30 P. M.

Temperance meeting Tuesday evening. Prayer-meeting Thursday evening.

There were reported last year 104 preaching services, with an attendance in the aggregate of 9,417 persons; 156 prayer-meetings, with an attendance in the aggregate of 7,809.

Thirteenth Ward, Lebanon Chapel, No. 70 Columbia street. Rev. James Marshall, pastor.

The Thirteenth Ward Mission was first commenced in 1854; removed to its present location, 1866. The church was organized in April, 1870. Sabbath services 10:30 A. M. and 7:30 P. M. Sabbath-school, 2 P. M. Weekly meetings Monday, Wednesday, and Friday evenings.

There were reported last year 58 preaching services, with an attendance in the aggregate of 5,800 persons; 180 prayer-meetings, with an attendance in the aggregate of 3,300 persons; and in the Sabbath-school 300 children received instruction.

Fourteenth Ward, Carmel Chapel, No. 134 Bowery. Rev. John Dooly, missionary in charge. Sabbath services 7:30 P. M. Prayer-meeting Friday evening. Daily prayer-meeting, 12 noon. Temperance meeting Monday evening.

There were reported last year 50 preaching services, with an attendance in the aggregate of 8,800 persons; 390 prayer-meetings, with an attendance in the aggregate of 31,530.

Seventeenth Ward, Olivet Chapel, No. 63 Second street, near Second avenue. Rev. A. F. Schauffler, pastor.

The Chapel was first opened for religious services, Sabbath evening, December 8, 1867; the Church was organized April, 1870. Sabbath services 11 A. M. and 7:30 P. M. Sabbath-school 11 A. M. and 2:30 P. M. Prayer-meetings Tuesday and Friday evenings.

There were reported last year 156 preaching services, with an attendance in the aggregate of 22,582 persons; 729 prayer-meetings, with an attendance in the aggregate of 28,254; and in the Sabbath-school 825 children received instruction.

The growth of Olivet Chapel may be seen in the figures following: The attendance upon the Sabbath morning service for several years has been as follows: in 1874, 74; in 1875, 92; 1876, 90; and in 1877, 106. The attendance Sabbath evening shows the average attendance in 1874, 117; 1875, 174; 1876, 204; and in 1877, 244. The Tuesday evening prayer-meeting for the same years shows 50, 65, 80, and 87. The Friday evening prayer-meeting shows 75, 91, 108 for the last three years. The Sabbath-school attendance has been 448, 514, 533, and 574 for the last four years, the ratio of attendance having doubled in the same time.

German Missions. Rev. Conrad Doench, pastor. German services, Sabbath at 10:30 A. M., and Thursday at 7:30 P. M., No. 70 Columbia street. Sabbath at 3 P. M., and Tuesday at 7:30 P. M., at No. 135 Greenwich street. Rev. Philip Jeblick, pastor. German services, Sabbath at 9:30 A. M., and Monday at 7:30 P. M., at No. 63 Second street.

There were reported last year 231 preaching services, with an attendance in the aggregate of 17,893 persons; 282 prayer-meetings, with an attendance in the aggregate of 16,928 persons; and in the German Sabbath-school 200 children received instruction during the year.

Helping Hand for Men, 316 Water street. Reading-room open daily; religious services every evening at 7:30; and on the Sabbath at 2:30 and 7:30 P. M.

THE CHURCHES.—In three of the chapels, the Christian ordinances have been introduced, and the total number of communicants enrolled in all, from the beginning, April, 1870, is 1,347. The number received last year is 147. The present number is 803.

## THE SERVICES.

**OLIVET CHAPEL, Rev. A. F. Schauffler, 63 Second Street.**
Prayer Meeting, Tues., 7:45 P.M. Boys' Meeting, Wed., 7:30 P.M. Mothers' Meeting, Friday, 3 P.M. Young People's Meeting, Friday, 8 P.M. Temperance Meeting, Tuesday, 7:30 P.M. SUNDAY SERVICES: 11 A.M., 7:30 P.M.; Song, 2 P.M., Sabbath-school, 2:30 P.M.

**CALVARY CHAPEL, Mr. W. F. Barnard, 153 Worth Street.**
Prayer Meeting, Thursday, 7:30 P.M. Bible Study, Friday, 7:30 P.M. Temperance Meeting, Monday, 7:30 P.M. SUNDAY SERVICES: Bible Class, 2 P.M., Singing, 7:30 P.M., Preaching, 7:45 P.M.

**LEBANON CHAPEL, Rev. James Marshall, 70 Columbia Street.**
Prayer Meeting, Wednesday, 7:30 P.M. Mothers' Meeting, Thursday, 3 P.M. Temperance Meeting, Monday, 7:30 P.M. SUNDAY SERVICES: S. S., 2:30 P.M., Adult Bible Class, 2:30 P.M., Preaching, 7:30 P.M.

**CARMEL CHAPEL, Rev. John Dooly, 134 Bowery.**
Prayer Meetings, Tuesday, Wednesday and Friday, 7:30 P.M. Daily Meetings, 12 noon. Temperance Meeting, Monday, 7:30 P.M. SUNDAY SERVICES: Special Prayer, 4 P.M., Preaching, 7:30 P.M.

**DE WITT CHAPEL, Rev. George Hatt, 135 Greenwich Street.**
Prayer Meeting, Thursday, 7:30 P.M. Temperance Meeting, Wednesday, 7:30 P.M. SUNDAY SERVICES: Preaching, 10:30 A.M. and 7:30 P.M., S. S., 9 A.M. and 1:30 P.M.

## CARMEL CHAPEL, 134 BOWERY.

The City Mission is making systematic efforts to carry the gospel to all persons, without respect to country, creed, color, sex, or age, and through its various instrumentalities reaches hundreds of thousands of all classes. In 1872, in conjunction with the Young Men's Christian Association, a building was leased in the Bowery, near Grand street, and fitted up in a neat and attractive manner as a chapel and reading-room. This chapel was first opened Sabbath evening, May 5, 1872, with a sermon by the Rev. Dr. John Hall. In September following, the Rev. A. F. Schauffler took charge of the work, and continued in office until called to the Olivet Chapel. Lately the Rev. D. Stuart Dodge has voluntarily given his time freely to the general oversight of the work. The Rev. John Dooly, the assistant missionary, may daily be found at the chapel.

The work of Carmel Chapel is almost exclusively among men—men who have come to the city in search of employment, and failing in this, and being without means or friends, are compelled to accept assistance. The statistics of the operations directly under the charge of the Young Men's Christian

Association for the last year, will indicate the usefulness of the work:

| | | | |
|---|---|---|---:|
| Total number | | Calls made and received | 9,430 |
| " | " | Letters written by visitors | 9,800 |
| " | " | Men sent to hospital | 59 |
| " | " | Visitors to Reading-room | 5,030 |
| " | " | Free lodgings | 8,941 |
| " | " | Different men lodged | 1,230 |
| " | " | Free baths | 1,498 |
| " | " | Garments given | 266 |
| " | " | Meals given | 39,998 |
| " | " | " sold | 55,197 |
| " | " | Situations furnished | 227 |
| " | " | Men registered | 675 |

The religious services under the immediate direction of Rev. D. Stuart Dodge are attended by large numbers, and many have given credible evidence of a radical change in heart and life. The general order of the meetings held in Carmel Chapel for the week is as follows:

Daily noonday Prayer-meeting 12 to 1 P. M.

Sabbath.—Meeting of Special Prayer, 4 P. M.; Preaching for the People, 7:30 P. M.

Monday.—Gospel Temperance Meeting, 7:30 P. M.

Tuesday.—Inquiry Meeting, 7:30 P. M.

Wednesday.—Young Men's Social Prayer-meeting, 7:30 P. M.

Thursday.—Entertainments, Readings, etc., when advertised.

Friday.—Prayer-meeting, 7 : 30 P. M.

Family Prayers in the Library every evening, 9 : 30.

For the six years Carmel Chapel has been open, the aggregate attendance has been as follows :

| | |
|---|---:|
| Temperance Meetings, (Pledges signed, 4,283) | 61,608 |
| Inquiry Meetings | 6,260 |
| Friday evening Prayer-meetings | 23,904 |
| Sabbath evening Preaching service | 38,834 |
| Noonday Prayer-meetings | 144,114 |
| Grand total | 274,720 |

The grand idea of Carmel Chapel is the preaching of the gospel, and the Executive Committee earnestly invite the attention of the friends and subscribers of the City Missions to the urgent necessity of sustaining this chapel, where the preaching of the gospel and other religious and moral services are regularly maintained, and where a large congregation is easily gathered. The necessary expenses for rent, missionary services, and incidentals must be provided for, and it is hoped that the evident usefulness of this work will encourage the wealthy and benevolent to furnish the means necessary to establish and endow it, and provide for the erection of a suitable building, commodious and attractive, which shall stand on the great thoroughfare as a permanent institution for the glory of God and the salvation of souls.

---

### OLIVET CHAPEL, NO. 63 SECOND STREET.

Seventeenth Ward, Olivet Chapel, No 63 Second street, near Second avenue, Rev. A. Schauffler, pastor.

The chapel was first opened for religious services, Sabbath evening, December 8, 1867; the church was organized April, 1870. Sabbath services, 11 A. M. and 7:30 P. M. Sabbath-school, 11 A. M. and 2½ P. M. Prayer-meetings Tuesday and Friday evenings.

There were reported last year 156 preaching services with an attendance in the aggregate of 22,582 persons; 729 prayer-meetings with an attendance in the aggregate of 28,254; and in the Sabbath-school 825 children received instruction.

The growth of Olivet chapel may be seen in the figures following: The attendance upon the Sabbath-morning service, for several years, has been as follows: in 1874, 74; in 1875, 92; in 1876, 90; and in 1877, 106. The attendance Sabbath evening shows the average attendance in 1874,

117; 1875, 174; 1876, 204; and in 1877, 244. The Tuesday evening prayer-meeting for the same years, shows 50, 65, 80, and 87. The Friday evening prayer-meeting shows 75, 91, 108, for the last three years. The Sabbath-school attendance has been 448, 514, 543, and 574, the last four years, the ratio of attendance having doubled in the same time.

The chapel is admirably divided into rooms of various sizes, all of which may be thrown open upon occasion, thereby adapting the accommodations to larger or smaller meetings, and to the various purposes of the mission. Let us see how the missionary work is carried on, and what is aimed at in the different means and agencies employed. We commence with the Sabbath. At $9\frac{1}{2}$ A. M. preaching in German; at 11 A. M. Bible-class exercises, which take the place of a preaching service and of the morning session of the Sabbath-school; at $2\frac{1}{2}$ P. M. the regular session of the Sabbath-school is held; at 4 P. M. a Sabbath school prayer-meeting; and at $7\frac{1}{2}$ P. M. the evening preaching service is held, which closes the Sabbath. Monday at $7\frac{1}{2}$ P. M. the German people meet for prayer and conference. Tuesday, at 2 P. M. the Helping Hand Association gather the poor women together to make up, at a fair compensation, useful garments for themselves and their families, which are afterwards sold to them at cost. The Association also provide a few groceries, which are retailed at wholesale prices. While the women are at work, familiar talks on household thrift and economy, and domestic management, and matters of sickness, health, etc., are entered upon by the pastor and other competent persons. At 7½ P. M. the regular weekly prayer-meeting is held. Wednesday, at 2 P. M. the pastor meets with his assistants and colaborers to look over the work, and seek by prayer and conference renewed strength and courage; at 7½ P. M. the Sabbath-school teachers meet for the study of the lesson. Thursday, at 2 P. M. the German Mothers' meeting is held. Friday, at 2 P. M., the English Mothers' meeting is held; at 7½ P. M. the young people meet for prayer and praise. Saturday, at 10½ A. M., the Children's prayer-meeting and sewing-school are held.

In Olivet Chapel there is a church organization, in which there have been enrolled 628 members, and a Sabbath-school of children and youth of 825 members. There is a Missionary Association, a Young People's Association, a Mutual Sewing Relief Association, a Helping Hand Association, and other auxiliaries for good.

## THE HELPING HAND AT OLIVET CHAPEL.

Helping women to help themselves is the best kind of help. While so many Christian workers are discussing the questions, "How to help the poor without pauperizing them," "How to prevent imposition," and "How to reach the masses," a band of women is quietly working out the problem in a down-town chapel.

Every Tuesday afternoon they meet for three hours, from half-past one. Every applicant for aid is visited and her case thoroughly investigated. If worthy, she is received, placed in a class, given a garment on which to sew, and a card prepared for the purpose, on which the account of her earnings is placed each week. Twelve cents an hour is the price paid for labor there. Good material is provided, and the garments must be well made. The women are permitted to order the garments most needed by them or their children, and if they wish can take half their pay in groceries.

Nearly three hundred, divided into classes of eight, have been employed this winter. Three-fourths of these are widows—many with families, and others, too old to work, yet unwilling to go to the almshouse, while soul and body can be kept together in any other way.

And while these prudent, efficient, and successful efforts are made to supply these women with work and wages, they are also furnished with the best religious instruction, and their social and moral wants met with kindness and care. Any interested in this work will be welcome at Olivet Chapel, 63 Second street, every Tuesday afternoon, and a few ladies who speak German will be invaluble.

Like all kindred institutions, this feels the pressure of the times. Though the applications are multiplied, the means have not increased in proportion. A separate fund is kept for the relief of special cases, and any donations for either the general work or the "Emergency Fund," will be gladly received and faithfully applied, if addressed to Mrs. M. K. Jesup, 197 Madison avenue, Mrs. David S. Egleston, 8 East Thirty-fifth street, or Mrs. A. R. Brown, 50 Bible House.

Helping Hands are also carried on, in connection with Lebanon Chapel and Calvary Chapel; that in the former place being supported and managed by ladies of the Presbyterian church, Englewood, N. J., Rev. Henry M. Booth, pastor.

## HONORARY MEMBERS.

Rev. Thos. E. Vermilye, D. D.
Rev. Wm. Adams, D. D.
Rev. Wm. R. Williams, D. D.
Rev. Mancius S. Hutton, D. D.
Rev. Stephen H. Tyng, D. D.
Rev. Edward D. Smith, D. D.
Rev. Edwin F. Hatfield, D. D.
Rev. Sam'l D. Burchard, D. D.
Rev. Thomas Armitage, D. D.
Rev. T. W. Chambers, D. D.
Rev. Wm. A. Hallock, D. D.
Rev. S. I. Prime, D. D.
Rev. Henry M. Field, D. D.
Rev. R. D. Hitchcock, D. D.
Rev. Wm. W. Newell, D. D.
Rev. George L. Prentiss, D. D.
Rev. E. P. Rogers, D. D.
Rev. W. G. T. Shedd, D. D.
Rev. T. D. Anderson, D. D.
Rev. S. D. Alexander, D. D.
Rev. Joseph Holdich, D. D.
Rev. Howard Crosby, D. D.
Rev. Robert R. Booth, D. D.
Rev. D.M.L. Quackinbush, D. D.
Rev. Enoch Van Aken.
Rev. John Cotton Smith, D. D.
Rev. Andrew Stevenson, D. D.
Rev. Thos. S. Hastings, D. D.
Rev. C. C. Norton.
Rev. E. A. Washburn, D. D.
Rev. James D. Wilson.
Rev. S. H. Tyng, Jr., D. D.
Rev. Julius W. Geyer.
Rev. David Gregg.
Rev. David Terry.
Rev. W. M. Paxton, D. D.
Rev. Wm. Ormiston, D. D.
Rev. A. A. Reinke.

Rev. W. T. Sabine.
Rev. John Hall, D. D.
Rev. G. S. Chambers.
Rev. N. W. Conkling, D. D.
Rev. A. C. Wedekind, D. D.
Rev. J. J. Brouner.
Rev. G. H. Mandeville, D. D.
Rev. R. H. Newton.
Rev. C. S. Robinson, D. D.
Rev. Henry M. Booth.
Rev. Wm. M. Taylor, D. D.
Rev. Edward L. Clark.
Rev. George H. Hepworth.
Rev. M. R. Vincent, D. D.
Rev. S. M. Hamilton.
Rev. S. B. Rossiter.
Rev. Halsey Moore.
Rev. J. S. Ramsay.
Rev. C. A. Stoddard, D. D.
Rev. George O. Phelps.
Rev. George S. Payson.
Rev. W. J. Tucker, D. D.
Rev. Erskine N. White, D. D.
Rev. F. H. Marling.
Rev. Joseph R. Kerr.
Rev. Carlos Martyn.
Rev. Alfred H. Moment.
Rev. Henry T. Hunter.
Rev. L. D. Bevan.
Rev. Arthur Brooks.
Mr. R. L. Stuart.
Mr. Samuel B. Schieffelin.
Mr. William Walker.
Mr. E. S. Jaffray.
Mr. James Lenox.
Mr. William E. Dodge.
Mr. Frederick Marquand.
Mr. William Libbey.

## OFFICERS.

### PRESIDENT.
### A. R. WETMORE.

### VICE-PRESIDENT AND TREASURER.
### MORRIS K. JESUP.

### CORRESPONDING SECRETARY AND ASSISTANT TREASURER.
### LEWIS E. JACKSON.

## DIRECTORS.

George W. Abbe.
Austin Abbott.
Benjamin B. Atterbury.
Josiah W. Baker.
George W. Beale.
Nathan Bishop.
Riley A. Brick.
James H. Briggs.
Albert N. Brown.
John S. Bussing.
William A. Cauldwell.
Charles C. Colgate.
John B. Cornell.
Hiram A. Crane.
Stephen Cutter.
Henry Day.
William E. Dodge, Jr.
Charles M. Earle.
David S. Egleston.
Ambrose K. Ely.
Zebulon S. Ely.
Lewis Hallock, M. D.
A. S. Hatch.
Robert Hoe.
James C. Holden.
Samuel Inslee, Jr.
David Irwin.
Joseph C. Jackson.
Thomas F. Jeremiah.
Morris K. Jesup.
John Taylor Johnson.
Joseph F. Joy.
Caleb B. Knevals.
Charles Lanier.
Joseph B. Lockwood.
Benjamin Lord.
George De F. Lord.
John R. Ludlow.
Walter T. Miller.
John E. Parsons.
Howard Potter.
Gamaliel G. Smith.
James T. Smith.
Roswell C. Smith.
Thomas Storm.
Thomas S. Strong.
John H. Washburn.
A. R. Wetmore.
Thomas W. Whittemore.
Jacob F. Wyckoff.

## EXECUTIVE COMMITTEE.

Rev. John Hall, D. D.
Rev. C. S. Robinson, D. D.
Rev. Wm. M. Taylor, D. D.
Rev. Wm. Ormiston, D. D.
Rev. Wm. J. Tucker, D. D.
Rev. D. Stuart Dodge.
A. R. Wetmore.
Nathan Bishop.
John Taylor Johnston.

Morris K. Jesup.
William E. Dodge, Jr.
Howard Potter.
A. S. Hatch.
Gamaliel G. Smith.
Walter T. Miller.
Ambrose K. Ely.
John E. Parsons.
Lewis E. Jackson.

## BUILDING COMMITTEE.

Morris K. Jesup.
John Taylor Johnston.
Howard Potter.
Ambrose K. Ely.
Gamaliel G. Smith.

## MISSIONARY COMMITTEE.

Rev. John Hall, D. D.
Rev. C. S. Robinson, D. D.
Rev. Wm. M. Taylor, D. D.
Rev. Wm. Ormiston, D.D.
Rev. Wm. J. Tucker, D.D.
A. R. Wetmore.

## FINANCE COMMITTEE.

A. R. Wetmore.
Morris K. Jesup.
William E. Dodge, Jr.
A. S. Hatch.
Howard Potter.

## AUDITORS.

Walter T. Miller.
Ambrose K. Ely.

The Corresponding Secretary is a member *ex-officio* of all the standing committees.

## MISSIONARIES.

1. Mr. Lewis E. Jackson, Sec., 50 Bible House.
2. Rev. George Hatt, 135 Greenwich street.
3. Mr. James Farrow, 135 Greenwich street.
4. Mr. W. F. Barnard, 153 Worth street.
5. Mr. John Anderson, 185 Spring street.
6. Rev. James Marshall, 70 Columbia street.
7. Mr. G. W. Martin, 70 Columbia street.
8. Rev. John Dooly, 134 Bowery.
9. Mr. John Ruston, 114 East 22d street.
10. Rev. A. F. Schauffler, 63 Second street.
11. Mr. Robert T. Listen, 63 Second street.
12. Mr. Eugene Peck, 63 Second street.
13. Rev. Conrad Doench, 132 Cannon street.
14. Rev. Philip Jeblick, 143 First avenue.
15. Mr. G. R. Lederer, 303 West 29th street.
16. Rev. Marinus Willett, 50 Bible House.
17. Mr. J. F. Patton, 2247 Second avenue.
18. Mrs. Lefler, 65 Orchard street.
19. Mrs. Ward, 70 Columbia street.
20. Mrs. Rogers, 194 Prince street.
21. Miss Vantine, 409 West 19th street.
22. Mrs. Van Morsten, 107 First avenue.
23. Mrs. Wisner, 63 Second street.
24. Miss McDonald, 50 Bible House.

## MISSIONARIES.

25. Miss Eighmey, 55 East Ninth street.
26. Mrs. Miller, 55 East Ninth street.
27. Miss Monroe, 55 East Ninth street.
28. Miss Smyth, 55 East Ninth street.
29. Miss Dye, 55 East Ninth street.
30. Miss March, 55 East Ninth street.
31. Miss Root, 50 Bible House.
32. Mrs. Miles, 155 Worth street,
33. Miss Dow, 55 East Ninth street.
34. Miss Gumbart, 55 East Ninth street.
35. Miss Miller, 55 East Ninth street.
36. Miss Post, 55 East Ninth street.
37. Mrs. Barnum, 55 East Ninth street.
38. Mrs. Sloat, 55 East Ninth street.
39. Mrs. A. R. Brown, Sup't Female Branch, 50 Bible House.

The missionary women in the foregoing list are appointed and supported by the Female Branch of the City Mission, and their labors are directed by the Female Superintendent in connection with the Executive Committee of the Female Branch.

### PRESENT STATUS OF THE GOSPEL WORK.

THIS Society has under its care 35 MISSIONARIES, who make 70,000 VISITS every year, carrying help, and sympathy, and comfort, and blessing to 20,000 FAMILIES who are outside of all parochial care.

The CITY MISSION gives the preaching of the gospel to 250,000 PERSONS during the year. Recently it has commenced the administration of the Christian ordinances in the Mission Chapels, so that now the people have pastoral care and instruction, and Christian fellowship and aid, and church government and discipline, as in regularly incorporated churches.

In THREE CHAPELS Christian communities have been organized on a simple union basis, the Apostles' Creed being the only symbol of faith, and more than 1,347 members in all have been enrolled.

The CITY MISSION gathers the children into Sabbath-schools wherever accessible, and supports 4 MISSION SABBATH-SCHOOLS, giving instruction and care to 2,000 children, mostly of the very destitute and needy class.

It also maintains Sewing Schools, Helping Hand Associations, Employment Societies, Temperance Organizations, Reading Rooms, Lodging Houses, and in every way that Christian love and ingenuity can devise, is seeking to carry the gospel to the poor and needy who are not reached by the churches.

TO SUPPORT THE MISSIONARIES, maintain the MISSION CHAPELS, and carry on 100 DIFFERENT SERVICES every week, and provide the TRUTH FOR DISTRIBUTION, only $50,000 per year is required. Properly and efficiently to reach the spiritual destitutions of the city, $100,000 or $200,000 could be advantageously used.

And the disbursement of the largest amount named would not involve the addition of a single dollar for office expenses or salaries. The ratio of expense is only $2\frac{1}{2}$ per cent. of the income, and the larger the capital the smaller the ratio of expense, the cost of administration being the same.

The Executive Committee of the City Mission, composed of pastors and laymen, give their personal attention to the management of affairs, and regularly inspect every department of the work.

MR. LEWIS E. JACKSON, Corresponding Secretary and Assistant Treasurer, collects the statistics, edits the reports and documents, and attends to the correspondence, the finances, and the general business of the Society.

The work of the Female Branch, an important auxiliary, is directed by MRS. A. R. BROWN, Superintendent.

The Annual Report of the City Mission, containing full accounts of all the churches and charities of the city, may be had on application at the office, 50 Bible House.

## CHURCH ORGANIZATION.

When a church is to be organized, the order of proceeding is as follows:

1. A committee of the Executive Committee shall be appointed to visit the mission chapel, and those persons who shall wish to unite in the Christian society there to be formed, shall present to this committee the evidence of their piety, either by certificate of their church membership, or by examination before the committee, and when approved by the committee they shall form the Christian Society of said mission.

2. The Society thus defined shall immediately proceed to elect, by a majority of all its members, in which of the forms recognized among evangelical Christians the ordinances shall be observed within it, and this decision shall be irreversible in that Society, except by a vote of three-fourths of all its members.

3. It shall then be submitted to the Society whether they will elect four or six officers, in classes of two each, to whom shall be committed

the duty of examining, under the counsel of the missionary in charge, and receiving all additional members, and of excluding from the ordinances those who, after a fair investigation, shall be found to be unworthy of them.

4. If such election be determined upon, it shall at once proceed. The officers of the second class then elected shall hold office for one year, when there shall be an election of an equal number of officers to take their place. The officers of the first class shall be replaced by an election to be held two years hence, and yearly elections shall be held thereafter, in such manner that all officers shall serve for two years. The officers who shall have completed their term of office shall be re-eligible.

5. These officers shall have a spiritual oversight of the members of the Society, but they shall have no control of any of those details of mission work which have hitherto been within the power of the Executive Committee. The discipline which they shall administer shall conform to rules to be hereafter drawn out by the Executive Committee.

6. When any convert who shall wish to join the Society thus constituted, shall have conscientious preferences in behalf of any form of baptism in use

among evangelical Christians, that ordinance shall be administered in his case according to such preference. And when so many as five members of such Society shall have conscientious preferences in behalf of any mode of administering the Lord's Supper, which is in use among evangelical Christians, and is different from that which has been chosen by the Society, a special communion-service, according to such preference, shall be appointed for them, to occur as frequently as the service adopted by the Society.

7. The ordinances shall in each case be administered by an ordained minister, who shall be connected with some evangelical ecclesiastical body in this city or vicinity.

8. The Apostles' creed shall be adopted by the Society above described.

## FORMS OF REPORTS.

### FORM OF REPORTING.
### FORM OF MISSIONARY REPORT.

---------------------------- Ward Report ---------------- 187 .

| Number of visits. | Number of tracts distributed. | Bibles and Testaments supplied to the destitute. | Vols. lent from ward libraries. | Children gathered into Sabbath-schools. | Children gathered into day-schools. | Persons gathered into Bible classes. | Persons induced to attend church and mission stations. | Temperance pledges obtained. | Preaching services held. | Prayer-meetings held. | Persons restored to church fellowship. | Missionary visits made. | Calls made and received. | Converts united with evangelical churches. | Families relieved. | Amount given. |
|---|---|---|---|---|---|---|---|---|---|---|---|---|---|---|---|---|
| | | | | | | | | | | | | | | | | |

### FORM OF FEMALE MISSIONARY REPORT.

**Assistant Missionary Report** ---------------- *Month* ---------- 187 .

| Number of tracts distributed. | Bibles and Testaments supplied to the destitute. | Vols. lent from ward libraries. | Children gathered into Sabbath-schools. | Children gathered into public schools. | Persons gathered in Bible classes. | Persons induced to attend church and mission stations. | Temperance pledges obtained. | Religious meetings held. | Persons restored to church fellowship. | Missionary visits. | Calls made and received. | Persons united with churches. | Families relieved. |
|---|---|---|---|---|---|---|---|---|---|---|---|---|---|
| | | | | | | | | | | | | | |

### FORM OF RETURN FOR CONVASSING A DISTRICT.

**City Missionary Census** ---------------- *New York,* ---------- 187 .

| Street. | Number. | NAME. | Adults. | Children. | Protestant. | Romanists. | Jews. | Univ., salists, etc. | Communicants. | Attending church. | Not attending church. | Children in Sabbath-schools. | Children not in Sabbath-schools. | Destitute. | Sick. | REMARKS. |
|---|---|---|---|---|---|---|---|---|---|---|---|---|---|---|---|---|
| | | | | | | | | | | | | | | | | |

## BENEVOLENT SOCIETIES—CORPORATE TITLES.

In the accompanying list only the leading general organizations are named. A more complete catalogue will be found in "Christian Work in New York," the Annual published by the City Mission and Tract Society.

American Board of Commissioners for Foreign Missions.
American Bible Society.
American Home Missionary Society.
American Missionary Association.
American Church Missionary Society of the Protestant Episcopal Church.
American Baptist Missionary Union.
American Female Guardian Society.
American Seamen's Friend Society.
American Tract Society.
American Sunday-school Union.
Association for Improving the Condition of the Poor in the City of New York.
Association for Respectable, Aged, Indigent Females in the City of New York.
Board of Foreign Missions of the Presbyterian Church in the United States of America.

## BENEVOLENT SOCIETIES. 197

Board of Home Missions of the Presbyterian Church in the United States of America.

Children's Aid Society in the City of New York.

Five Points House of Industry, in the City of New York.

Home for Fallen and Friendless Girls, in the City of New York.

Howard Mission and Home for Little Wanderers, in the City of New York.

Missionary Society of the Methodist Episcopal Church.

National Temperance Society and Publication House.

New York City Mission and Tract Society.

New York City Mission and Tract Society for the Benefit of the Female Branch.

New York City Mission and Tract Society for the Christian Workers' Home.

New York Juvenile Asylum.

New York Magdalen Benevolent Society.

New York Society for the Relief of the Ruptured and Crippled.

Prison Association of New York.

Society for Promoting the Gospel among Seamen in the Port of New York, usually called the Port Society.

Wilson Industrial School for Girls, in the City of New York.

Woman's Aid Society, in the City of New York.

Woman's Hospital of the State of New York.

Young Men's Christian Association of the City of New York.

Young Women's Christian Association of the City of New York.

In this enumeration is presented a fair representation of the more prominent charities of the city, such as any good citizen might choose to remember in his will. Of course there are many other worthy objects, and there are societies, and boards, and institutions in connection with particular religious denominations, which could not be brought into this brief compass. Without disparaging any other benevolent enterprise, it may be said that it is believed that a careful examination of the work of City Evangelization will encourage the wealthy and benevolent not only to contribute generously to its support from year to year, but will also lead them to remember the cause in their wills. A sum sufficient to endow a bed in a Hospital, or in a Home for Incurables, or to create an Emergency Fund, or to establish a Missionary Sanitarium, would be of great service to the cause. A legacy of $50,000 will provide for the erection of a Mission Chapel, which would become a fitting memorial of the testator, and stand on some of the city thoroughfares, as a permanent institution for the glory of God and the salvation of souls.

Legacies of any amount will be acceptable, and will be used in forwarding the objects of city evangelization, or devoted to any special purpose designated by the testator. The form to be used in making bequests will be found below:

---

FORM OF A BEQUEST TO THE CITY MISSION.

I give and bequeath to "THE NEW YORK CITY MISSION AND TRACT SOCIETY," instituted in the City of New York, and incorporated by the Legislature of the State of New York, the sum of _____dollars to be applied to the charitable uses and purposes of said Society.

A general form of bequest is added, which may be used for any other benevolent society, by filling in the blanks:

## GENERAL FORM OF A BEQUEST.

I bequeath to my executors the sum of ............ dollars, *in trust*, to pay over the same in ............... after my decease, to the person who, when the same is payable, shall act as treasurer of the ..................... Society, formed in ..................... in the year eighteen hundred and ............... to be applied to the charitable purposes of said Society and under its direction.

www.ingramcontent.com/pod-product-compliance
Lightning Source LLC
Chambersburg PA
CBHW021732220426
43662CB00008B/820